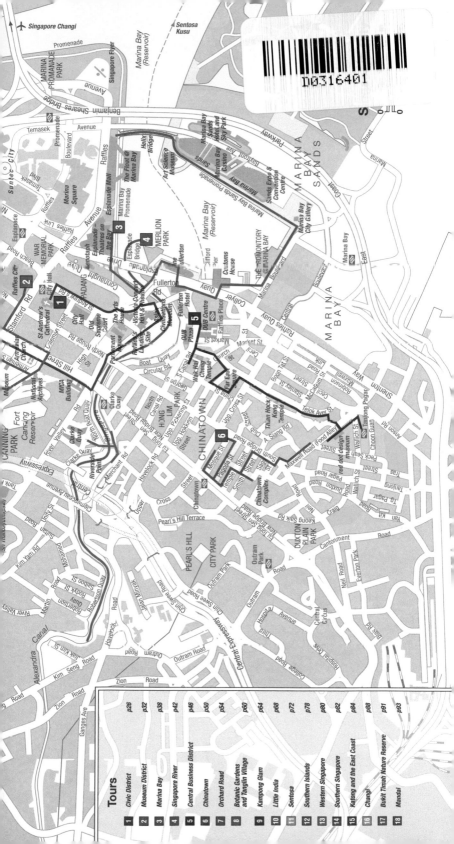

Tours

1	Civic District	p26
2	Museum District	p32
3	Marina Bay	p38
4	Singapore River	p42
5	Central Business District	p46
6	Chinatown	p50
7	Orchard Road	p54
8	Botanic Gardens and Tanglin Village	p60
9	Kampong Glam	p64
10	Little India	p68
11	Sentosa	p72
12	Southern Islands	p78
13	Western Singapore	p80
14	Southern Singapore	p82
15	Katong and the East Coast	p84
16	Changi	p88
17	Bukit Timah Nature Reserve	p91
18	Mandai	p93

CONTENTS

Introduction
About this Book   4
Recommended Tours   6

Overview
City Overview   10
Food and Drink   14
Shopping   18
Nightlife   20
History: Key Dates   22

Walks and Tours
1. Civic District   26
2. Museum District   32
3. Marina Bay   38

4. Singapore River   42
5. Central Business
     District   46
6. Chinatown   50
7. Orchard Road   54
8. Botanic Gardens
     and Tanglin Village 60
9. Kampong Glam   64
10. Little India   68
11. Sentosa   72
12. Southern Islands   78
13. Western Singapore   80
14. Southern Singapore 82
15. Katong and
     The East Coast   84

16. Changi   88
17. Bukit Timah
     Nature Reserve   91
18. Mandai   93

Directory
A–Z   98
Accommodation   110
Restaurants   116
Nightlife   122

Credits and Index
Picture Credits   124
Index   126

Above from top: orchids at the National Orchid Garden; trinkets in Chinatown; resident at the Jurong BirdPark; Raffles Hotel; laksa, a local hawker staple.

ABOUT THIS BOOK

This *Step by Step Guide* has been produced by the editors of Insight Guides, whose books have set the standard for visual travel guides since 1970. With top-quality photography and authoritative recommendations, this guidebook brings you the very best of Singapore in a series of 18 tailor-made tours.

WALKS AND TOURS

The walks and tours in this book are designed to provide something to suit all budgets, tastes and trip lengths. As well as covering Singapore's many classic attractions, the tours track lesser-known sights and up-and-coming areas in the city centre. There are also excursions for those who want to extend their visit and explore slightly further afield.

The tours embrace a range of interests, so whether you are an art fan, an architecture buff, a gourmet, a shopper, a nature lover or have children to entertain, you will find an option to suit.

We recommend that you read the whole of a tour before setting out. This should help you to familiarise yourself with the route and enable you to plan

where to stop for refreshments – options for this are shown in the 'Food and Drink' boxes, recognisable by the knife and fork sign, on most pages.

For our pick of the walks and tours by theme, consult Recommended Tours For... *(see pp.6–7)*.

OVERVIEW

The tours are set in context by this introductory section, which gives an overview of the city to set the scene, plus background information on food and drink, shopping and nightlife. A succinct history timeline in this chapter highlights the key events that have shaped Singapore over the centuries.

DIRECTORY

Also supporting the tours is a Directory chapter, comprising a user-friendly, clearly organised A-Z of practical information, our pick of where to stay while you are in the city and select restaurant listings; these eateries complement the more low-key cafés and restaurants that feature within the tours, and are intended to offer a wider choice for evening dining.

The Author

Malaysia-born Amy Van has lived in Singapore for over a decade. Not only does she call the city home, she counts it as one of her favourite places. Formerly the editor of a leading Singapore-based food and wine magazine, Amy is now a freelance contributor to a variety of food, travel and lifestyle publications, as well as international travel guides. She has also worked on numerous book projects as editor and stylist.

Margin Tips
Shopping tips, handy hints, information on activties, key historical facts and interesting snippets help visitors make the most of their time in Singapore.

Feature Boxes
Notable topics are highlighted in these special boxes.

Key Facts Box
This box gives details of the distance covered on the tour, plus an estimate of how long it should take. It also states where the route starts and finishes, and gives key travel information such as which days are best to do the route or handy transport tips.

Route Map
Detailed cartography shows the itinerary clearly plotted with numbered dots. For more detailed mapping, see the pull-out map slotted inside the back cover.

Food and Drink
Recommendations of where to stop for refreshment are given in these boxes. The numbers prior to each restaurant/café name link to references in the main text. On city maps, restaurants are plotted.

The $ signs at the end of each entry reflect the approximate cost of a meal for one, excluding drinks and taxes. These should be seen as a guide only. Price ranges, also quoted on the inside back flap for easy reference, are as follows:

$$$$	over S$50
$$$	S$30–50
$$	S$10–30
$	below S$10

Footers
Those on the left-hand page give the itinerary name, plus, where relevant, a map reference; those on the right-hand page show the main attraction on the double page.

THE ARTS

Take in a music or theatre performance at The Arts House (walk 1) or The Esplanade – Theatres on the Bay (walk 3). Spot public sculptures in the CBD (walk 5), check out the galleries in MICA Building (walk 1), and sample Southeast Asian art in the Singapore Art Museum (walk 2).

RECOMMENDED TOURS FOR...

FAMILIES WITH CHILDREN

Sentosa (tour 11) has plenty of attractions to keep the little ones entertained. At the Jacob Ballas Children's Garden (walk 8) and the Science Centre (tour 13), curious minds will be amply satisfied.

PARKS AND GARDENS

Escape the urban jungle to the lush forest in the Bukit Timah Nature Reserve (walk 17) or opt for a leisurely walk through the landscaped Botanic Gardens (walk 8). See gorgeous orchids in Mandai (tour 18) or the National Orchid Garden (walk 8).

FOODIES

Foodies won't be disappointed with the Singapore-style seafood in the East Coast (walk 15) and the hawker offerings in the Amoy Street Food Centre (walk 5), Maxwell Road Food Centre (walk 6), Chinatown Food Street (walk 6) and Taman Serasi Food Garden (walk 8).

NIGHTLIFE

Cool, understated bars flourish in Tanglin Village (walk 8), while Clarke Quay's (tour 4) and St James Power Station's (tour 14) flashy clubs are great for all-night partying. Sentosa (tour 11) has laid-back beach bars and jazz fans should head to Boat Quay (tour 4) and Kampong Glam (walk 9).

WILDLIFE

The city's animal parks impress with their naturalistic habitats and conservation focus. Set aside a day for the Singapore Zoo and Night Safari (tour 18) and make a trip to the Jurong BirdPark (tour 13).

SHOPAHOLICS

Mall-hop on Orchard Road (walk 7), browse idiosyncratic shops in Kampong Glam (walk 9) and Ann Siang Hill (walk 6), comb Chinatown (walk 6) and Little India (walk 10) for cultural finds, and indulge in buying sprees in Suntec City (walk 3) and VivoCity (walk 14).

ARCHITECTURE

Don't miss the iconic Esplanade – Theatres on the Bay (walk 3). View grand colonial-era buildings in the Civic District (walk 1), skyscrapers designed by superstar architects in the CBD (walk 5) and flamboyant Peranakan terrace houses in Emerald Hill (walk 7) and Katong (walk 15).

LOCAL CULTURE

Explore the city's eclectic cultures in its ethnic neighbourhoods (walks 6, 9 and 15). For a glimpse into the Straits Chinese way of life, wander around Katong (walk 15) or visit the Peranakan Museum (walk 2).

HISTORY BUFFS

For windows onto Singapore's past, cruise down the historic Singapore River (tour 4) or view age-old places of worship in the CBD (walk 5). Visit history museums in the Museum District (walk 2) and Sentosa (tour 11) or venture east to the Changi Prison Chapel and Museum (walk 16) for reminders of the Japanese Occupation.

OVERVIEW

An overview of Singapore's geography, customs and culture, plus illuminating background information on food and drink, shopping, nightlife and history.

CITY OVERVIEW   10

FOOD AND DRINK   14

SHOPPING   18

NIGHTLIFE   20

HISTORY: KEY DATES   22

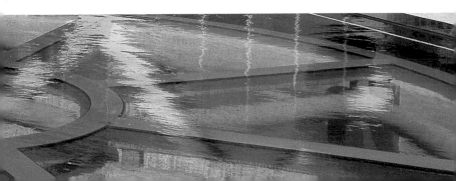

CITY OVERVIEW

The small city-island state of Singapore has huge attractions, laudable achievements and even grander ambitions. These superlatives are impressive, but more memorable are its warm, eclectic people, ethnic neighbourhoods, and its simple joys of food, shopping and nightlife.

For some, Singapore is merely a welcome stopover, its top-rated airport making it the perfect gateway to Southeast Asia. For others, this tiny island, with its legendary cleanliness, widespread use of English as well as celebrated sights, shops, eateries and colourful ethnic neighbourhoods, is an appealing destination in its own right; an ideal introduction, in fact, to all of Asia in one fell swoop.

DEVELOPMENT

In 1819 Englishman Thomas Stamford Raffles from the British East India Company founded modern Singapore. Recognising the potential of this tiny blip of an island shrouded in jungle and swamp and occupied only by Orang Laut (Sea People), a few Malay families and some Chinese traders, he went on to set up a trading post. He ordered the land to be cleared, supervised an ambitious construction campaign, and welcomed labourers and merchants from China, India and all over Southeast Asia. His free-trade policies soon created a boomtown of 10,000 residents, at which some 2,000 ships called annually. In short, Raffles laid the groundwork for the vibrant free port of Singapore that remains in place today.

Multilingual City
Four official languages are used in multicultural Singapore: English, Mandarin, Malay and Tamil. The language of administration is English, which is also the lingua franca. On the streets, you will hear different languages and dialects being spoken, including Singlish, a patois that combines English, Malay and Chinese dialects, which most Singaporeans identify with.

Right: bird's-eye view of the Civic District, with the Asian Civilisations Museum in the foreground.

Modern-Day Singapore

Singapore's modern-day visionary was Lee Kuan Yew, the first prime minister. Under the direction of Lee and his successors, Goh Chok Tong and Lee Hsien Loong, Singapore has continued to be one of Southeast Asia's brightest stars over the past four decades. The government's paternal approach has defused racial and labour disputes, its public housing schemes have provided most citizens with their own homes, and its savvy economic policies have attracted foreign trade and investment.

Its invasive social engineering policies – from banning smoking in public places and outlawing the sale of chewing gum, to monitoring flushing in public toilets and imposing huge taxes on car ownership – may have drawn sneers from the Western media, but Singapore is undeniably the cleanest and most orderly of all Asian cities. What some Westerners perceive as draconian laws and little personal freedom in an authoritarian state, are regarded by many pragmatic Singaporeans as merely the common-sense way to run a country.

ORIENTATION

Located at the southern tip of peninsular Malaysia, Singapore consists of the main island, 699 sq km (270 sq miles) in area, and 63 other smaller islands. Most of the main island is less than 15m (50ft) above sea level, and the highest point is Bukit Timah Hill, at 163.63m (537ft).

Downtown Singapore remains largely arranged according to the original town plans Raffles had executed in 1819. The colonial hub of the city, today's Civic District, is still the heart of the administration, as it was in Raffles' time. The clamour of Chinatown and the hum of business in the Central Business District around Raffles Place have not diminished. The Muslim area of Kampong Glam and the predominantly Hindu Little India retain their ethnic feel. Chic Orchard Road, a plantation area in colonial times, has been transformed into one of Asia's premier shopping belts.

Conservation

When Singapore achieved independence in 1965, the economy was in shambles. Like many other developing nations, it put urban renewal and economic progress on the front burner; anything that stood in the way, from historic neighbourhoods to colonial architecture, was simply razed. As a result, by the 1970s it had achieved

Above from far left: enjoy breathtaking views onboard the Singapore Flyer – the world's tallest observation wheel; Garden City Singapore.

Singapore Story For an insight into Singapore's meteoric rise, read *The Singapore Story*, the vivid and fascinating memoirs of Lee Kuan Yew, who, whether you like him or not, has been credited with bringing the country to where it is today.

Public Housing

In land-scarce Singapore, providing housing for the masses means building skywards. More than 80 percent of Singaporeans own and live in high-rise flats built by the Housing and Development Board. In many other parts of the world, public housing is associated with poverty and social unrest, but not in Singapore. Its public housing programme is in fact one of its finest achievements, with other fast-growing countries seeking to emulate its success.

Climate
The temperature ranges between 27°C (80°F) and 33°C (91°F), and dips slightly during the northeast monsoon season between November and February.

prosperity, but was criticised for its lack of character and culture.

In the 1980s the authorities began to restore buildings in four conservation areas: Boat Quay, Little India, Kampong Glam and Chinatown/Tanjong Pagar. Since then, more temples, buildings, shophouses and warehouses have been spared the wrecking ball. The gentrification, apart from giving the city added charm, has also helped Singaporeans develop a sense of their own history, although some feel that the preservation efforts have come too late.

A Garden City
Singapore packs in quite a bit despite its minuscule size. Once you have covered the city centre, venture out to the suburbs, where the housing heartlands are interspersed with quirky theme attractions as well as forest reserves and other pockets of greenery.

Below: the city's transport system and infrastructure is modern and efficient.

The city's vast green zones surprise many first-time visitors, at least those expecting to find a sterile and air-conditioned metropolis of glass and steel. There is a legion of green belts, such as parks nestled between skyscrapers, offering respite in the concrete jungle. Four gazetted nature reserves, namely Central Catchment, Bukit Timah, Sungei Buloh and Labrador together comprise over 3,340 hectares (8,250 acres) of untouched greenery – which is by no means slim pickings for this land-scarce city.

Getting Around
Street signs are clear and the city is relatively easy to navigate. The various districts can be easily explored by bus, Mass Rapid Transit (MRT) trains or on foot, although the weather can get hot, humid and possibly uncomfortable for some. Taxis are comfortable, inexpensive and especially good for journeys to destinations in the suburbs.

A MELTING POT

Singapore has about 5.08 million people, comprising 74.1 percent Chinese, 13.4 percent Malays, 9.2 percent Indians, with the remaining 3.3 percent made up of Eurasians, Arabs, Jews and other minority groups.

The lingua franca is English, but on the streets you will see Chinese, Malay, Indian, Eurasian and Caucasian faces. Singapore has been a migrant society since day one, and continues to receive new immigrants from the world over today. Mosques, churches, and Hindu

and Chinese temples often stand side by side, and cuisines borrow ideas and ingredients willy-nilly from one another.

Preoccupations

The country tends to be overly competitive, thanks to a *kiasu* (meaning 'afraid to lose' in the Chinese Hokkien dialect) attitude. It is always in a big hurry to chase grand dreams and strive for success, and has already made itself the world's busiest port and the second largest oil refiner, as well as home to the globe's best airline and airport. The ambition to be No. 1 in everything it does is perhaps driven by a sense of insecurity and the need to get the attention of and connect to the world beyond its limited shores, though a positive side to this is that the city has become one well-oiled, efficient machine.

Keeping up with the Joneses is also a major preoccupation of Singaporeans. At housewarming parties queries on the cost of the house and renovation are earnestly entertained. A compliment on a nice watch or a piece of jewellery will almost always be followed by a question on its price and provenance. If you are asked questions on money, don't be fazed; no rudeness or intrusiveness is intended. You could even think of it as cultural exchange.

Pastimes

When removed from their workaday world and indulging in their favourite pastimes, Singaporeans do let up and and have fun. Without a doubt, the most well-loved activity is eating. The island's cultural diversity has given it a mind-boggling array of food options; as a result, this city never stops eating, even into the wee hours of the morning. Shopping ranks only a close second as Singaporeans' favourite diversion. Many indefatigable locals have been known to trawl Orchard Road on the weekends, mall by mall.

A CHANGING CITY

Singaporeans joke that if they leave the country for more than three months, they will not be able to recognise many places on their return. So relentless is the pace of change.

Today the city is undergoing a renaissance of epic proportions. A new financial district and a revitalised waterfront has given it an extra boost and tourist arrivals have been increasing, thanks to the opening of two casino resorts – known as Integrated Resorts – and a Universal Studios theme park.

This city, once derided as boring, is also learning to take itself less seriously. Its nightlife scene swings with cool bars and clubs, both imported and home-grown. And if the vibrant arts calendar is anything to go by, its appetite for high culture is definitely growing.

But change is manifest not only in the physical landscape. If some of the people you meet seem less than gracious despite the national kindness campaign, it is often because they are in a hurry, under the constant pressure to change for the better, 'upgrade' and improve themselves. For many, time is perhaps the greatest luxury in the rush for a better future.

Above from far left: the Changi Airport is consistently rated the world's best; a Chinese mother and child enjoying a meal at East Coast Park; the Esplanade Theatre in Marina Bay; the buzzing Marina Bay promenade.

FOOD AND DRINK

Singapore's cultural diversity has resulted in a vibrant food scene and a veritable explosion of flavours. With a mind-boggling array of options that cater to different tastes and budgets, you will never leave the island hungry.

Eating Out
It is possible to dine out at every meal, 365 days of the year, yet not go back to the same place twice on this tiny island. There is a staggering number of eateries, from the truly exquisite at fine-dining restaurants to authentic local delicacies at no-frills, but no less worthy, hawker centres.

Eating is a great passion in Singapore and life revolves around food. Singaporeans talk about food all the time and debate on where to get the freshest crabs, the spiciest chilli sauce or the best chicken rice – for hours on end and preferably over a meal. At the many food courts and hawker centres peppered all over the island, you can sample different cuisines in a single venue freshly cooked by an array of vendors.

Every imaginable cuisine is represented on this island, from refined Japanese and piquant Korean to robust Thai and exotic Middle Eastern. There are also excellent fine-dining restaurants, including Modern European, and traditional French and Italian, all with impressive wine lists to match.

CHINESE CUISINE

For just Chinese cuisine alone, a wide range of authentic restaurants can be found in Singapore – including those that serve the regional cuisines of China and food of different dialect groups.

Delicate dim sum, double-boiled soups and roasted meats are prepared in the Cantonese kitchen, while hearty meat dishes are rustled up by Hokkien cooks. Refined Teochew dishes usually comprise light, wholesome flavours such as steamed seafood, comforting rice porridge and clear soups. The Hakkas are famous for their *yong tau fu* or beancurd stuffed with fish paste, and home-spun dishes flavoured with potent home-made rice wine.

The tongue-numbing Sichuan and robust Hunan food, both known for their liberal use of hot chilli peppers, as well as strongly flavoured Shanghainese and fine Beijing dishes are some of the many regional cuisines one can savour here.

INDIAN CUISINE

The Indian kitchen is largely divided into South and North Indian. South Indian meals mainly consist of fiery curries, aromatic *biryani* rice cooked with meat or seafood, as well as vegetarian *thosai* (rice pancakes) served with lentils. Several Indian restaurants in Singapore are well known for serving spicy southern fare on banana leaves.

North Indian cuisine is famous for its flavoursome tandoor grills, mild and rich curries, as well as fluffy *naan* breads. Meanwhile, the Keralan table, although not as well known, features a host of lip-smacking seafood dishes.

Indian chefs often use a blend of spices such as cardamom, cloves, cumin and coriander to enliven their dishes. Yoghurt is sometimes added to North

Indian curries to temper the spices, whereas coconut milk is used to mellow the intensely hot South Indian ones.

A hybrid Indian-Muslim food is usually found in hawker stalls around the island. Some familiar specialities are *roti prata* (a flaky griddle-fried bread eaten with curry), as well as *murtabak* (like *roti prata*, but stuffed with shredded chicken or mutton, sliced onions and egg).

MALAY CUISINE

Singaporean Malays are descendants of settlers from the Malayan Peninsula or Indonesia's Java and Sumatra islands. Mention Malay cuisine and one usually thinks of *nasi padang* (rice and assorted meat and vegetable side dishes) and spicy curries. These dishes usually include an assortment of spices and herbs such as ginger, turmeric, galangal, lemongrass, curry leaves, chillies and the ubiquitous *belacan* (a pungent shrimp paste). These dishes are often balanced with coconut milk, which takes the edge off the heat.

Nasi padang originates from Padang in West Sumatra. The many *nasi padang* eateries dotted around the island usually offer a wide variety of spicy meat and vegetable dishes served with white or turmeric-flavoured rice. At hawker centres, satay is a perennial favourite at Malay stalls. Aromatic bamboo skewers of marinated beef, mutton or chicken are grilled over hot charcoal and served with sliced onion, cucumber, rice cakes and a piquant spicy and sweet peanut sauce.

PERANAKAN CUISINE

A unique cuisine that deserves special mention is Peranakan, or Nyonya, cooking. Peranakans are descendants of early immigrants from China who settled in 19th-century Penang, Melaka and Singapore and married local Malay women. Peranakan cuisine originates from the fusion of Malay and Chinese culinary styles.

To impart a distinctive flavour and aroma to their rich curries and stews, chefs add the essential *rempah* mixture – fragrant herbs and spices such as lemongrass, chillies, shallots, candlenuts, *belacan* (shrimp paste) and turmeric ground by hand in a pestle and mortar. Tamarind paste, coconut milk and *taucheo* (fermented beans) are

Above from far left: South Indian fare features fiery-hot dishes; dim sum is an all-time lunch favourite for many.

Peranakan Food Scattered in the Katong neighbourhood are longstanding restaurants serving Peranakan delights. Especially notable is Kim Choo's glutinous rice dumplings (see p.85), ideal for a light breakfast.

Below: hotel chefs serve local hawker fare too.

Above from left:
roti prata, Hainanese chicken rice and satay – local delicacies that are readily available across the island.

Satay
Every evening, Boon Tat Street beside the Lau Pa Sat Festival Market becomes a pedestrian-only street and is transformed into an atmospheric haunt for satay lovers. Hawkers grill skewered meat over burning charcoal and serve them with rice cakes and a tangy peanut sauce dip.

Below: most seafood restaurants serve the mouthwatering chilli crab dish.

also used to liven up the robust concoctions. Dishes often require long hours of slow cooking and complicated preparations; flavours are complex and can range from fiery to delicate.

Desserts in the form of little cakes called *nyonya kueh* are colourful, sweet and sticky – perfumed with coconut cream and pandan leaves, and sweetened with dark and syrupy palm sugar.

Although best eaten in a Peranakan home, the food can be enjoyed in a handful of restaurants in Singapore. Look out for dishes such as *ayam buah keluak*, which combines chicken with earthy Indonesian black nuts to produce a rich, thick gravy as well as beef *rendang*, a spicy, dry beef stew that is often simmered for hours until fork tender.

SINGAPORE SIGNATURES

Over the years, several unique delicacies have evolved to tantalise the local tastebud. These dishes are particularly close to the hearts of Singaporeans.

Hainanese Chicken Rice

This iconic dish was first introduced by Hainanese immigrants from China. Succulent and juicy chicken meat poached in stock is served with fragrant rice that has been steamed with ginger, garlic and chicken stock. The chicken and rice are then served with delicious dips – vinegary chilli sauce, ginger paste and sweet black soy sauce.

Fish-Head Curry

This speciality is unique to the Indian community. Massive fish heads are stewed in a gravy alongside eggplant, tomatoes and okra. The meat is succulent and the gravy, spicy and intense. Aficionados say the cheeks, lips and eyes are the best parts of the fish head.

Chilli Crab

Singaporeans will tell you that this dish is best made with giant Sri Lankan crabs. The thick, tangy and spicy gravy is mopped up with fried or steamed *mantou* (Chinese buns).

Laksa

Thick rice noodles bathed in a rich and spicy coconut gravy jazzed up with herbs, and crowned with sliced fish cake, tofu, cockles, prawns and beansprouts.

BREAKFAST

A typical Singaporean breakfast usually means heading to a coffee shop for a dose of freshly grilled *kaya* toast –

bread spread with butter and a sweet coconut jam made from sugar, eggs and coconut cream, and flavoured with pandan leaves. To complement the stacks of crispy *kaya* toast, one can also order soft-boiled eggs drizzled with soy sauce and a cup of thick black coffee.

DRINKS AND DESSERTS

An iconic drink is *teh tarik* or 'pulled tea'. Tea sweetened with condensed milk is poured from cup to pitcher and back again to ensure that the concoction is well mixed and frothy. A variation is the soothing *teh halia* or ginger tea, a staple at Indian drink vendors. In hawker centres and at food courts, try freshly squeezed fruit juice, cold soya bean milk or sugar cane juice served with a wedge of lemon.

Delicious food needs something worthy to wash it down with, and the locally brewed Tiger and Anchor beers are excellent choices. Don't leave without tasting a Singapore Sling – a zesty blend of gin, cherry brandy, Cointreau, pineapple juice and fresh lime.

To end your meal, try *cendol* or *ice kacang* – shaved iced desserts with red beans and jelly, topped with syrup and coconut milk or evaporated milk.

HAWKER CENTRES

Hawker centres are scattered all over the island. Always a hive of activity, the scores of Malay, Chinese and Indian stalls offer a wide variety of traditional fare at cheap prices that will not bust your budget. Some of the most popular hawker centres are Lau Pa Sat Festival Market, Maxwell Road Food Centre and Newton Food Centre. From dawn till dusk, row upon row of stalls bustle with hawkers dishing out their specialities. Regulars often throng these places in search of their favourite stalls.

The local hawker centres are always packed during lunch and dinner, so head there earlier if you don't have the patience or time to wait for a table. However, communal sharing of tables is common during busy hours – simply smile and ask the person at the table if you can share it.

Getting Seats
If you are with a group at a hawker centre, have one person sit at a table to reserve the seats. The others, having noted the table number, should order their food and tell the hawkers where they are seated at.

Cookery Classes

There are a handful of established cookery schools in Singapore. at-sunrice (28 Tai Seng Street, Lift Lobby 2, Level 5; tel: 6416 6688; www.at-sunrice.com) offers demonstrations, tasting classes and hands-on cooking classes on Asian cuisine. Cookbook author Shermay Lee, at Shermay's Cooking School (Chip Bee Gardens, Blk 43 Jalan Merah Saga, #01-76; tel: 6479 8442; www.shermay. com), imparts Peranakan secrets based on her grandmother's traditional recipes. Coriander Leaf Cooking Studio (3A Merchant Court, #02-12 River Valley Road, Clarke Quay; tel: 6732 3354; www.corianderleaf.com) has lessons on Asian and Middle Eastern cuisines. Celebrity Chef Sam Leong and his wife Forest have set up Sam.Leong@ForestCooking School (4A Craig Road; tel: 6222 3305) in a quaint shophouse in Tanjong Pagar. Classes include Chinese cooking with a twist and Thai dishes.

SHOPPING

Singapore's shopping scene is hot. New malls sprout at breakneck speed while older ones receive makeovers. The choice ranges from Orchard Road's shiny, glitzy shopping centres to charming shophouses in the ethnic enclaves.

A Great Sale
There are no distinct sales periods that follow the seasons. Stores generally mark down their prices periodically. The best time to shop is from late May to early July during the annual Great Singapore Sale. Post Christmas and Chinese New Year are also good for bargains.

Shops are generally open daily from 10–11am to about 9pm, so you can literally shop till you drop. Some malls in Orchard Road open till late on Friday and Saturday nights.

SHOPPING DISTRICTS

Orchard Road

Orchard Road is to Singapore what Fifth Avenue is to New York. Even people who have never been to Singapore have heard of Orchard Road – such is its claim to shopping fame. The area is a shopaholic's dream – one dazzling mall after another filled with swanky department stores and any number of retail outlets and designer boutiques. There are malls dedicated to young children (**Forum The Shopping Mall**), pimply adolescents (**Far East Plaza** and **The Heeren**), antique and carpet fiends (**Tanglin Shopping Centre**) and the moneyed (**Hilton Gallery**, **Palais Renaissance**, **Ngee Ann City** and **The Paragon**), along with the usual shopping centres selling all manner of goods.

Marina Bay

The mega-sized **Suntec City Mall** has countless shops selling clothes, shoes, bags, electronic equipment, books and sports apparel. Adjoining it is a subterranean shopping mall called **CityLink**

Mall, which conveniently connects to the City Hall MRT station, **Marina Square** and the **Esplanade Mall**, part of the Esplanade – Theatres on the Bay.

The Shoppes at Marina Bay Sands is the latest addition to this area, with over 800,000 square feet of retail and restaurant space. Indulge in a unique luxury shopping experience; brands include Hermès, Chanel, Fendi and Gucci.

Civic District

Funan DigitaLife Mall is the place to find computer equipment and software. Above the City Hall MRT station is **Raffles City**, a six-storey mall with a wide array of retail outlets. Just opposite on North Bridge Road is **Raffles Hotel Shopping Arcade**, with a clutch of designer boutiques.

Kampong Glam

Arab Street is where to go for fabrics and handwoven baskets. The shops here are piled high with leather bags, baskets and rattan goods, purses and shoes. **Haji Lane**, lined with vintage boutiques and local designers' shops, is one of Singapore's hippest shopping streets.

Little India

Serangoon Road and the neighbouring side streets are a treasure trove of spices, jewellery, Indian silk and

more from the subcontinent. **Mustafa Centre** at Syed Alwi Road is a large 24-hour shopping mall crammed with low-priced electronic goods and other bargains. **Little India Arcade** comprises colourful restored shophouses stuffed with interesting paraphernalia.

Chinatown

For all things Chinese, visit the tiny shops along Pagoda Street and Temple Street and the stalls at the **Chinatown Night Market**. Nearby **Yue Hwa Emporium** sells exquisite Chinese silk and handicrafts like teapots and fans.

WHAT TO BUY

Cameras and Audio Equipment

Prices are attractive, particularly for photographic equipment and MP3 players. Best to get an international guarantee, but if you want to take a risk on imported goods intended only for the local market, you can save on the price.

Computer Equipment

Being such a wired country, Singapore is a good place to purchase both hardware and software. The law comes down hard on bootleg software and frequent raids are carried out at shopping malls specialising in computers – so buy the genuine stuff and ask for a guarantee.

Watches and Jewellery

Watches are sold tax-free, and the choice is endless. Gold jewellery is also a good buy. Traditional designs crafted in 22K yellow gold are available at jewellers in Serangoon Road and Chinatown, while more contemporary pieces in 18K white or yellow gold set with precious or semi-precious stones are sold at local chains like Gold Heart and Lee Hwa in the shopping centres. International jewellers like Tiffany and Cartier have boutiques in Singapore too.

More unique are orchid blooms – sold under the Risis brand – plated with 22K gold to preserve their beauty and crafted into jewellery.

Fashion and Accessories

Home-grown fashion designer Ashley Isham has his own plush store at Mandarin Gallery and Orchard Central. Other local names of note are project-shopbloodbros, M)Phosis and Bodynits.

Antiques and Asian Handicrafts

The range of antiques and handicrafts from Bangkok, Borneo and beyond is vast. There are baskets from the Philippines, Buddha images from Myanmar, Indian brassware, Chinese ceramics and more. Ask for a certificate of authenticity if you buy the genuine stuff.

Above from far left: handwoven carpets at Kampong Glam; Orchard Road shop display.

Sales Tax
There is a 7 percent Goods and Services Tax (GST) on most purchases in Singapore, for which tourists can claim refund for purchases above S$100.

Below: gold-plated orchid blooms from the Risis brand make unique souvenirs and jewellery pieces.

NIGHTLIFE

Once described as bland and banal, the island's nightlife scene has gone up a few notches on the hip index in recent years. Whether it's a no-holds-barred night of pub-crawling, clubbing or bopping, the choices are diverse.

Pricey Booze
Expect to pay S$10 or more for a pint of beer and S$12 for house pours. Premium beers cost about S$15–20 a pop, and a bottle of bubbly around S$100. All bills are tagged with a 10 percent service charge and 7 percent tax. Take advantage of happy hour discounts or one-for-one deals, usually from 5 to 9pm.

Information
Magazines such as *Juice* and I-S are good sources for nightlife and event listings. These are free and can be picked up at various cafés and nightspots. Websites such as e-clubbing (www. e-clubbing.com*)* also offer information on the clubbing scene.

Party-goers in Singapore are a capricious lot, so the scene reciprocates with overwhelming variety and venues that open (and close) at a furious rate, though established hotspots continue to pack in the crowds year after year. There are alfresco bars on rooftops and by beaches; chic lounges for the design-conscious set; microbreweries that craft their own ales; pubs with live rock performances; dance clubs that rank among the best in the world; and multi-venue establishments that offer the gamut of entertainment.

WHERE TO GO

Nightspots are scattered all over the island, but there are a few key areas where you can spend an entire night hopping from one venue to another.

Singapore River
The nightlife hubs along the river are a quick taxi ride from one another. The bars and pubs set in conservation shophouses on **Boat Quay** are popular with tourists and executives from nearby Raffles Place. Upriver from Boat Quay, **Clarke Quay**, arguably the island's hottest after-hours destination, sizzles with fashionable people in flashy bars and clubs set in restored 19th-century warehouses.

Orchard Road
The main shopping strip of **Orchard Road** is home to classy hotel lounges and bars with live performances. At its southern end is **Emerald Hill**, which has charming pubs patronised by expats and creative types.

Sentosa and Surroundings
The beachside bars dotted on the island resort of **Sentosa**, such as **Café del Mar** and **Tanjong Beach Club**, are fantastic places for knocking back cocktails. Opposite Sentosa and adjacent to VivoCity shopping mall is **St James Power Station**, a massive entertainment complex with nine clubs and bars housed in a former coal-fired power station.

Further Afield
A number of fashionable nightspots are also worth exploring in more secluded enclaves. One prime example is **Dempsey Hill**, located near Singapore Botanic Gardens, where you will find some stylish al fresco bars and restaurants housed in former British army barracks and set amid lush greenery. The area is popular with both locals and tourists who want to spend a more relaxed evening away from the maddening crowds of the city centre.

HOTEL BARS

If you don't fancy a noisy street of bars and clubs, hotel bars are good alternatives. Swissôtel the Stamford has the vertigo-inducing **New Asia Bar** on its 71st floor, while Raffles Hotel's **Long Bar** is the progenitor of the gin-based Singapore Sling. Another good option is the smart **Post Bar** at the Fullerton Hotel; its menu includes a dizzying array of martinis. The Grand Hyatt's plush **Martini Bar** is also a top draw for its range of alcoholic concoctions.

CLUBS

Zouk, on Jiak Kim Street, is the island's most well-known dance club. It is part of the international clubbing circuit and plays a diet of edgy underground and house music. **Attica/Attica Too**, at Clarke Quay, are homegrown favourites where DJs spin everything from hip-hop to electronic beats. **Butter Factory** at One Fullerton is another popular clubbing hotspot among the trendy set.

LIVE ENTERTAINMENT

For such a tiny city, Singapore has a fantastic range of live entertainment.

Rock/Pop Music
The best places to listen to Singapore musicians and bands are **The Pump Room** at Clarke Quay, **Timbré** at The Substation and **Wala Wala Café Bar** in Holland Village. They perform pop and rock covers as well as original works.

Jazz
For an evening of jazz, head to Boat Quay's **Harry's Bar** or Arab Street's **Blu Jazz Café**. These have line-ups of local bands as well as international jazz acts.

Classical Music
The **Singapore Symphony Orchestra** performs mainly mainstream classics at their weekly concerts at the **Esplanade Concert Hall**.

Theatre and Dance
Singapore's lively English-language theatre scene sometimes features a mix of Broadway favourites and musicals like *The Lion King* as well as local productions of original works. Companies to watch include **Wild Rice**, **Theatre-Works**, **The Necessary Stage** and **Singapore Repertory Theatre**.

The dance scene is headlined by the **Singapore Dance Theatre**, whose repertoire ranges from the classics to contemporary ballet set to pop music. Another company to look out for is **Arts Fission**, whose edgy productions draw inspiration from Asian heritage.

HISTORY: KEY DATES

From a tiny fishing village to a pivotal trading post at the crossroads of the East and West to the Asian economic powerhouse it is today, Singapore's evolution is nothing short of its inhabitants' ingenuity and hard work.

BRITISH COLONIAL RULE

1819	Sir Stamford Raffles sets up a trading post for the British East India Company with the agreement of the Sultan of Johor and the Temenggong, his representative on the island.
1824	The Sultan cedes Singapore in perpetuity to the British.
1826	Singapore, with Malacca and Penang, becomes part of the Straits Settlements, under the control of British India.
1867	The Colonial Office in London takes over control of Singapore.
1911	The population of Singapore grows to 250,000 and the census records 48 races on the island, speaking 54 languages. It becomes the greatest naval base of the British empire east of Suez.
1942	The Japanese invade and occupy Singapore.
1945	The Japanese surrender and the Allied Forces return.

POST-WORLD WAR II

Bleak Sight
Upon his arrival in Singapore in 1819, Sir Stamford Raffles found 'all along the beach... hundreds of human skulls, some of them old but some fresh with the hair still remaining, some with the teeth still sharp, and some without teeth.'

1946	Singapore becomes a Crown Colony.
1948	The British allow limited elections to the Legislative Council. A state of emergency is declared in June, following the Malayan Communist Party's uprising against British imperialism.
1951	Singapore is formally proclaimed a city with a royal charter.
1955	The Rendel Constitution granted by the British leads to general elections; David Marshall is appointed chief minister.
1956	People's Action Party (PAP) Central Executive Committee elections, in which the Communists decline to run, are held. Chinese students riot; PAP leaders are arrested.
1958	Singapore is granted partial independence.
1959	At the first general elections for a Legislative Assembly, PAP's Lee Kuan Yew becomes prime minister.
1963	Singapore joins the Federation of Malaysia.
1964	PAP wins only one seat in the Malaysian general elections. Racial riots take place.

POST-INDEPENDENCE

1965   Singapore withdraws from the Federation and becomes a republic. It joins the United Nations and the Commonwealth.

1967   Singapore, Malaysia, Thailand, Indonesia and the Philippines form the Association of Southeast Asian Nations (ASEAN).

1968   In the first general elections, PAP wins all 58 seats.

1971   The remaining British troops in Singapore leave.

1987   The US$5 billion Mass Rapid Transit (MRT) system opens.

1990   Lee Kuan Yew steps down after 31 years as prime minister and hands the reins over to Goh Chok Tong. The constitution is amended to provide for an elected president.

1991   PAP wins the elections, but loses four seats to the opposition in their poorest showing at the polls since 1959.

1993   Ong Teng Cheong is Singapore's first elected president.

1999   S.R. Nathan from the minority Indian race is appointed president.

21ST CENTURY

2002   The landmark Esplanade – Theatres on the Bay opens. Al Qaeda-linked terrorist plot to bomb the US embassy uncovered. Some 15 suspects are arrested and jailed without trial.

2003   Outbreak of Severe Acute Respiratory Syndrome (SARS) in April. The North-East Line extension of the MRT opens.

2004   Lee Hsien Loong is Singapore's third prime minister.

2006   PAP wins the general elections, taking 66.6 percent of the votes.

2008   The Singapore Flyer, the world's tallest observation wheel, opens. Singapore wins the bid to host the inaugural Youth Olympics in 2010. The world's first Formula 1 night race is held in September. Marina Barrage, Singapore's first reservoir in the city, opens.

2009   Singapore hosts the Asia-Pacific Economic Cooperation (APEC) meetings. The first stations in the MRT's Circle Line extension open in May.

2010   Singapore's first Integrated Resort, Resorts World Sentosa, opens in January, while the second one, Marina Bay Sands, opens in April. The first Youth Olympic Games (YOG) are held in August.

2011   The general elections are held in May and the ruling People's Action Party (PAP) wins with their lowest ever ratings of 60 percent. Soon after, 87-year-old founding father Lee Kuan Yew announces his retirement from cabinet.

Above from far left: ancient map of the Malay archipelago; the Singapore River in the 1900s.

Literary Greats
Colonial Singapore played host to many literary lions of the British empire, such as Somerset Maugham and Rudyard Kipling, who penned down their impressions of the island. Maugham wrote: 'The Malays, though natives of the soil, dwell uneasily in the towns, and are few. It is the Chinese, supple, alert and industrious, who throng the streets; the dark-skinned Tamils walk on their silent, naked feet, as though they were but brief sojourners in a strange land… and the English in topees and white ducks, speeding past in motor cars or at leisure in their rickshaws, wear a nonchalant and careless air.'

WALKS AND TOURS

1. Civic District — 26

2. Museum District — 32

3. Marina Bay — 38

4. Singapore River — 42

5. Central Business District — 46

6. Chinatown — 50

7. Orchard Road — 54

8. Botanic Gardens
   and Tanglin Village — 60

9. Kampong Glam — 64

10. Little India — 68

11. Sentosa — 72

12. Southern Islands — 78

13. Western Singapore — 80

14. Southern Singapore — 82

15. Katong and
    the East Coast — 84

16. Changi — 88

17. Bukit Timah Nature Reserve — 91

18. Mandai — 93

CIVIC DISTRICT

Many of the historical buildings in the Civic District have been restored and adapted for contemporary functions, but the genteel colonial elegance of the area remains unmistakable.

DISTANCE 2.5km (1½ miles)
TIME Half a day
START St Andrew's Cathedral
END Raffles Hotel
POINTS TO NOTE
Take the MRT to the City Hall station and turn left after the fare gates. This brings you to the side entrance of St Andrew's Cathedral. If you take a taxi, ask the driver to stop at the taxi stand in front of the Peninsula Shopping Centre.

Shopping
Facing St Andrew's Cathedral is the I.M. Pei-designed Raffles City, a vast complex comprising a shopping mall, the 72-storey Swissôtel the Stamford and the 26-storey Fairmont Singapore. Beneath the complex is the City Hall MRT station, which is linked via the subterranean CityLink Mall to Suntec City and the Esplanade – Theatres on the Bay *(see p.39)*.

In his town plan of 1822, Stamford Raffles designated the area north of the Singapore River as the colonial hub, ordering the building of offices, banks, hotels, churches and clubs. The area, roughly between the City Hall and Dhoby Ghaut MRT stations, is now known as the Civic District.

ST ANDREW'S CATHEDRAL

Start at the graceful **St Andrew's Cathedral ❶** (tel: 6337 6104; daily 7am–7.30pm). This English Gothic-style church was built by Indian convict labourers, who used a special plaster known as Madras *chunam*, made of egg white, egg shells, lime, sugar and coconut husk, to achieve the gleaming white exterior. The structure you see now is actually the second church to be built on this site, designed by Ronald MacPherson and consecrated in 1862. The earlier Palladian-style building was struck by lightning twice and demolished in 1852.

Church Highlights
Architecturally significant and steeped in history, the cathedral has, befittingly, been gazetted as a national monument. Note the pretty stained-glass windows behind the altar. Known as the East Windows, the three panels are dedicated to Stamford Raffles, John Crawfurd, the second resident of Singapore, and Major General William Butterworth, a governor of the Straits Settlement. Behind the pulpit is the Coventry Cross, formed by nails salvaged from the ruins of England's Coventry Cathedral, which was destroyed during World War II.

THE PADANG

A diagonal path leads from the cathedral to the green expanse known as the **Padang ❷** ('field' in Malay), along St Andrew's Road. Known as the Esplanade in colonial times, this was where the Europeans played cricket and socialised in the cool of the

evenings. In 1942, during the Japanese Occupation, European civilians were rounded up on the Padang and forced to march 22km (14 miles) to Changi, where they were imprisoned. Today the Padang plays host to public events and rugby and cricket matches.

On either side of the Padang are private clubs, the venerable Victorian-style **Singapore Cricket Club** to your right and the newer **Singapore Recreation Club** to your left.

CITY HALL

Across St Andrew's Road from the Padang are two handsome structures that used to be Singapore's most important government buildings. In 1945 Lord Louis Mountbatten accepted the Japanese surrender on the grand staircase of the **City Hall ❸**, which was completed in 1929. It was also here, in front of the grand Grecian columns, that Lee Kuan Yew declared Singapore's self-government status in 1959 and the country's independence in 1963.

Court Buildings

Next to the City Hall is the green-domed **Old Supreme Court ❹**, built in 1939. Of note is the tympanum sculpture by Italian sculptor Cavalieri Rudolfo Nolli. He is said to have used his daughter as his model for the centre figure of Justice, which is flanked by figures representing a lost soul, the law, gratitude, prosperity and abundance.

The Old Supreme Court and City Hall buildings are currently being converted into the **National Art Gallery**

(www.nationalartgallery.sg), which will open progressively from the end of 2014. Looming right behind is the glass-and-steel **New Supreme Court ❺**, capped by a futuristic disc. The observation deck on the 8th floor (free) has good views of the city.

VICTORIA THEATRE AND CONCERT HALL

Cross Parliament Place and past the Old Parliament House to the **Victoria Theatre** and **Victoria Concert Hall ❻**,

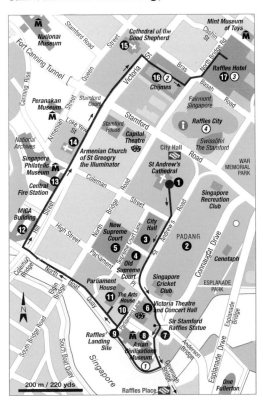

200 m / 220 yds

Peranakan Museum
The former wing of Asian Civilisations Museum at Armenian Street has been converted into the Peranakan Museum *(see p.33)*, a fine repository of Straits Chinese artefacts and antiques.

Below: the statue of Raffles at the Raffles' Landing Site.

which are linked by a landmark clock tower. (Both are closed for renovations until 2013.) Although the two neoclassical buildings were designed to match, the theatre, completed in 1862 as a town hall, predates the 1902 concert hall. They are now much eclipsed by the newer venues at The Esplanade –Theatres on the Bay *(see p.39)*, but remain important performing spaces.

Raffles' Statue

For the centenary of Singapore's founding in 1919, a bronze **statue of Sir Stamford Raffles ❼**, cast by T. Woolner, was relocated from the Padang to the Victoria Memorial Hall, now the Victoria Concert Hall. It was moved to the National Museum during World War II and thereafter returned to the forecourt of the concert hall in 1946.

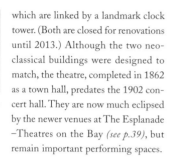

ASIAN CIVILISATIONS MUSEUM

From the theatre and concert hall, move on to the **Asian Civilisations Museum ❽** (tel: 6332 7798; www. acm.org.sg; Mon 1–7pm, Tue–Sun 9am–7pm, Fri 9am–9pm; charge) on Empress Place. Designed in neoclassical style by J.F. McNair, the original building was completed in 1865. Be sure to devote enough time to this wonderful museum with 11 galleries. Its diverse collection of artefacts, from prehistoric agricultural tools to textiles and bronzeware, reveal Asia's cultural and historical complexities.

Gallery Highlights

In the China Gallery, displays such as Chinese deities and fragile Dehua porcelain are the highlights, while the Koran-inspired calligraphic art in the West Asia Gallery is impressive. The South Asia galleries hold religious statuary and architectural motifs of the Indian subcontinent.

After your museum tour, head to the riverfront **Siem Reap II**, see ⑪①, for lunch. If not, there are more dining options later in the tour.

RAFFLES' LANDING SITE

Continue on the leafy promenade by the Singapore River to the **Raffles' Landing Site ❾**. Here stands another statue of Stamford Raffles, a white marble replica of the original in front of the Victoria Concert Hall, which marks the spot on the northern bank

Above from far left: Southeast Asian gallery at the Asian Civilisations Museum; the Chamber at The Arts House.

where the man first stepped ashore on 28 January 1819. There are fine views of Boat Quay *(see p.43)* and the Central Business District *(see p.46)* across the river.

THE ARTS HOUSE

Adjacent to the Raffles' Landing Site is **The Arts House ⑩** (tel: 6332 6900; www.theartshouse.com.sg; Mon–Fri 10am–8pm, Sat 11am–8pm; free), a multidisciplinary arts centre occupying the former Parliament House, which was built in 1827. The building was originally designed to be the private residence of a wealthy merchant. It was instead used as the first Court House and Assembly House, and then by the Parliament until 1999. In its grounds is a bronze elephant statue, a gift from King Chulalongkorn of Siam in 1871.

The Arts House has a busy schedule of film screenings, art exhibitions, and theatre and dance performances. Its 200-seat performance space, named the Chamber, was where members of parliament debated bills and laws in the past. Today they parley at the austere **Parliament House ⑪** just behind.

MICA BUILDING

If you decide to call it a day, cross Cavenagh Bridge to the Raffles Place MRT station. If you are keen to explore the Civic District further, then walk by the riverside to Elgin Bridge; on its right is an underpass that takes you to North Boat Quay. Cross the road to Hill Street, on which stands

the **MICA Building ⑫**, the Renaissance-style headquarters of the Ministry of Information, Communications and the Arts. The building, erected in 1934 with 911 technicoloured window shutters, used to be the Old Hill Street Police Station. On its ground floor is the **ARTrium**, with several art galleries showcasing the works of local and Asian artists.

Fort Canning Park
Turn left as you exit the MICA Building and walk along Hill Street. Next to the building is a steep staircase, which leads up to the **Fort Canning Park** *(see p.32)*.

CENTRAL FIRE STATION

Further along is the **Central Fire Station ⑬**, the oldest fire station in Singapore, housed in a fine example of the 'blood and bandage' architectural style, completed in 1901. This style, with alternating exposed brickwork and whitewashed plaster, is a departure from the usual Palladian and classical styles prevailing in Singapore at the time.

Singapore Design
The Shop at The Arts House (tel: 6337 1086; www.thearts house.com.sg; Mon–Sat 11am–8pm) features inspired homeware, jewellery, pottery and illustrations from Singapore artists and designers.

Food and Drink 🍽

① SIEM REAP II
Asian Civilisations Museum; tel: 6338 7596; www.indochine. com.sg; daily 11am–11pm; $$
A contemporary café serving Indochinese specialities such as rice paper rolls, salads and *pho* (Vietnamese beef noodle soup). The trendy Bar Opiume *(see p.122)* next door is a hotspot for pre- and post-dinner drinks.

Above from left: outside the Civil Defence Heritage Gallery; cloister at Chijmes; the Armenian Church; garden in the grounds of the Armenian Church.

Civil Defence Heritage Gallery

The fire station also houses the **Civil Defence Heritage Gallery** (tel: 6332 2996; www.scdf.gov.sg; Tue–Sun 10am–5pm; free), a unique museum with displays of antique fire engines and interactive stations depicting fire-fighting operations. On the guided tour, you get to climb up the hose tower, the lookout point in the early days.

ARMENIAN CHURCH

Across Coleman Street from the fire station is the **Armenian Church of St Gregory the Illuminator ⑭** (tel: 6334 0141; daily 9am–6pm), the oldest church in Singapore built in 1835. This is where Singapore's small Armenian community congregates on Sunday. In its memorial garden lie the tombstones of prominent Armenians in Singapore's history. Among them are the tombstones of the Sarkies brothers who founded the Raffles Hotel, and Agnes Joaquim, who discovered the orchid hybrid *Vanda Miss Joaquim*, now Singapore's national flower.

CATHEDRAL OF THE GOOD SHEPHERD

At the intersection of Victoria Street and Bras Basah Road on the left is the **Cathedral of the Good Shepherd ⑮** (tel: 6337 2036; Mon–Fri 7am–5.30pm, Sat until 7.30pm, Sun 7.30am–7pm), the oldest Roman Catholic church in Singapore and a national monument. Completed in 1846, it was designed by Denis Lesley Sweeney. Its architecture recalls that of England's St Martin-in-the-Fields and St Paul's in Covent Garden. The three bells in the steeple were cast by the Auguste Hildebrand Foundry in Paris. Originally hung for swing chiming, they have since been replaced with electric tolling hammers. In its grounds is the residence of the current Archbishop of Singapore, a simple two-storey bungalow with a portico and enclosed verandahs.

CHIJMES

Opposite the cathedral across Victoria Street is the restaurant and entertainment hub **Chijmes ⑯** (tel: 6337 7810; www.chijmes.com.sg), pronounced 'chimes'. The Gothic-style buildings were formerly occupied by the Convent of the Holy Infant Jesus (CHIJ), founded in 1854. The Sisters on the

---

Food and Drink 🍴

② JAPANESE DINING SUN
02-01 Chijmes; tel 6336 3166; daily noon–3pm, Mon–Sat 6.30pm–11pm, Sun 6pm–10.30pm; $$
Authentic Japanese dishes and beautifully presented modern interpretations as well as light, delicate desserts. Opt for the fuss-free lunch sets if the menu is too mind-boggling.

③ AH TENG'S BAKERY
Raffles Hotel; tel 6412 1816; Sun–Thur 11am–10pm, Fri, Sat 11am–11pm; $$
This cosy old-school café is excellent for afternoon tea. On the menu are local snacks, dim sum and cakes.

④ CANELÉ
B1-81 Raffles City Shopping Centre; tel: 6334 7377; www.lesamis.com.sg; daily 10am–10pm; $$
Canelé is famous for its selection of fine French-style pastries, cakes and ice creams. The menu also offers salads, sandwiches, pastas and dessert crêpes.

Seine from France ran a school with boarding facilities for girls and an orphanage, which took in babies left at its Gate of Hope on Victoria Street.

The conversion of a convent school and religious building into a nightlife hub was not without controversy, but it is generally agreed that the restoration was tastefully done; the mouldings in the chapel and along the walkway are especially beautiful, and the fountain courtyard is a pleasant place for a pause. Peek into the old chapel, which has exquisite stained glass; it is now used for dinners and concerts. Speciality shops and restaurants line the cloistered walkways.

A good place for lunch here is **Japanese Dining Sun**, see ⑪②.

RAFFLES HOTEL

Exit Chijmes at the intersection of Bras Basah and North Bridge roads. Diagonally opposite Chijmes is the last stop of your tour, the legendary **Raffles Hotel** ⑰ (tel: 6337 1886; singapore.raffles.com). Built in 1887 by the Sarkies brothers and restored in the 1990s, the hotel has welcomed famous personalities over the years. Somerset Maugham summed up its spirit best when he said the 'Raffles stands for all the fables of the exotic East'. The genteel air of this national monument is still palpable today and is best soaked up in the leafy courtyard with antique fountains. If you are interested in the hotel's history, visit the **museum** (tel: 6337 1886; daily 10am–7pm; free), which has a collection of Raffles mem-

orabilia. The **shopping arcade** has bespoke tailors, antiques stores, and luxury boutiques of brands like Tiffany & Co., Coach and Louis Vuitton.

Night time Raffles

The Raffles Hotel has good options for the night. There may be performances at its **Jubilee Hall**. After dinner at one of its many restaurants, have a quiet drink at the **Bar & Billiard Room**, which carries a nice selection of cigars, and still has the very billiard table under which, so the story goes, the last tiger in Singapore was shot. For something less formal, there is the raucous **Long Bar**, the only place in Singapore where you can toss peanut shells onto the floor with impunity.

But for now, after your tour of the Raffles, have tea at **Ah Teng's Bakery**, see ⑪③, or at **Canclé**, see ⑪④, in Raffles City across Bras Basah Road.

Singapore Sling
This was first created as a lady's cocktail in 1910 by Chinese bartender Ngiam Tong Boon at the Long Bar in the Raffles Hotel. Various versions exist today, but the one served at the Long Bar is modified from the original, which calls for gin, cherry brandy and Benedictine in equal parts, mixed with club soda.

Mint Museum of Toys

Across from the Raffles Hotel, on Seah Street, is the Mint Museum of Toys (tel: 6339 0660; www.emint.com; daily 9.30am–6.30pm; charge), a trove of rare toys, from vintage Popeye the Sailor and Felix the Cat to superheroes like Batman and Superman, put together by Chang Ya Fa, who started his collection when he was just six years old. To date he has accumulated some 50,000 pieces, estimated to be worth S$5 million, from auctions and curio shops around the world.

MUSEUM DISTRICT

Tiny Singapore has a disproportionally large number of museums, located all over the island. Thankfully for the visitor, the major ones, such as the National Museum, Peranakan Museum and Singapore Art Museum, are conveniently clustered in the Civic District in a zone known as the Museum District.

Above:
remains of the
old gates at Fort
Canning Park.

DISTANCE Varies, depending on
the number of museums visited
TIME A full day
START The Battle Box
END Singapore Art Museum
POINTS TO NOTE
Take the MRT to the City Hall station
and head first to the Raffles City
Shopping Centre for breakfast.

Among Singapore's many museums, there are historical ones that catalogue the island's early stories through artefacts and war relics; art and design museums that showcase cutting-edge creativity; and quirky repositories that display unique tastes. This tour brings you to four museums, each offering different insights into the city's heritage.

A good breakfast option in the area is **Cedele Depot**, see Ⓨ①, in Raffles City. After breakfast, exit the mall and walk down Stamford Road, past **Stamford House** which is currently being re-developed.

Turn left onto Hill Street, pass the Armenian Church *(see p.30)* and turn right onto Canning Rise, which brings you to **Fort Canning Park** on Fort Canning Hill.

THE BATTLE BOX

Behind the whitewashed Fort Canning Centre is **The Battle Box ❶** (tel: 6333 0510; www.legendsfortcanning.com/fortcanning/battlebox.htm; daily 10am–6pm, last entry 5pm; charge includes compulsory guided tour). The bunker, with a maze-like complex of rooms and corridors 9m (30ft) underground, was constructed in 1936 as the nerve centre of British military operations in Southeast Asia.

The Battle Box is now a museum chronicling the fall of Singapore to the Japanese during World War II through exhibitions created with audio and visual effects, animatronics and lifelike waxwork. It was here on 15 February 1942 that British officers made the decision to surrender. Adjacent to The Battle Box is a 1926 building that served as an army bar-

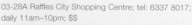

Food and Drink 🍴

① CEDELE DEPOT
03-28A Raffles City Shopping Centre; tel: 6337 8017;
daily 11am–10pm; $$
This outlet of a home-grown bakery chain serves great all-day breakfast. Fill up with the hearty Big Breakfast Set with brioche or white toast, bacon, sausages, scrambled eggs and mushrooms. No less decadent are the wild blueberry pancakes with vanilla butter and maple syrup, and the chocolate French toast.

racks; it now houses Hotel Fort Canning and **The Legends Fort Canning Park country club**.

FORT CANNING HILL

If time permits, explore Fort Canning Park on its well-marked paths. History abounds on Fort Canning Hill, once known as Bukit Larangan (Forbidden Hill) as commoners were not allowed here. Archaeological excavations indicate that the Malay princes who ruled Singapore in the 14th century had sited their palaces here. Stamford Raffles also built his residence here in 1823, as the hill offered good vantage for keeping watch on Singapore's coast. In 1860 the British built a fort here, from which dawn, noon and dusk each day were announced by cannon fire.

The hill also holds an old tomb said to contain the remains of Iskandar Shah, the last ruler of pre-colonial Singapore. This has been consecrated as a Muslim *keramat* (shrine).

Walk down the patch of green known as **Fort Canning Green**, which used to be an old Christian cemetery until 1865, towards the entrance that is marked by two Gothic gates. Leave the park and walk down Canning Rise towards Coleman Street, past the Registry of Marriages. The **Singapore Philatelic Museum** ② *(see margin)* is on your left. Turn onto Armenian Street.

PERANAKAN MUSEUM

On Armenian Street is the **Peranakan Museum** ❸ (tel: 6332 7591; www.peranakanmuseum.sg; Mon 1–7pm, Tue–Sun 9am–7pm, Fri until 9pm; charge), the first in the world dedicated to Peranakan heritage and material culture. Peranakans, or Straits

Above from far left: waxwork exhibit at The Battle Box; Peranakan Museum.

Stamp Museum
The Singapore Philatelic Museum (tel: 6337 3888; www.spm.org.sg; Mon 1–7pm, Tue–Sun 9am–7pm; charge) offers a unique window onto Singapore's history It has displays of postcards, first-day covers and stamps from the private collections of renowned philatelists.

Old School
The building that houses the Peranakan Museum was formerly occupied by the Tao Nan School. Set up by Hokkien immigrants to preserve their cultural heritage, it was the first school in Singapore to use Mandarin as the medium of instruction.

[Map showing Fort Canning Park area with labels: Dhoby Ghaut, Orchard Road, Singapore Management University, Bras Basah Street, Y.M.C.A., Fort Canning Road, Bras Basah, Waterloo St, Singapore Art Museum, Queen Street, The Legends Fort Canning Park, Percival Rd, Fort Canning Tunnel, National Museum ⑤ Ⓜ ②, Singapore Management University, Stamford Rd, Cathedral of the Good Shepherd, The Battle Box ❶, Fort Canning Centre, FORT CANNING GREEN, Canning, Fort Canning Link, Singapore Management University, Victoria Road, Chijmes, Raffles Hotel, FORT CANNING PARK, Reg. of Marriages, The Substation ④, Peranakan Museum Ⓜ ❸, Armenian Street, Loke Lew St, Stamford Street, Stamford Road, North Bridge Rd, Raffles The Plaza, Raffles City, Fort Canning Reservoir, Rise, Armenian Church, Burhani Mosque, Hill Street, Stamford House, Capitol Building, City Hall, Swissôtel The Stamford ❶, Singapore Philatelic Museum Ⓜ ②, St Andrew's Cathedral, 200 m / 220 yds, N]

Above: Peranakan *kamcheng* pot.

Chinese, have a fascinating hybrid culture that evolved over years of intermarriage between immigrant Chinese men and local Malay women since the 17th century in the former British Straits Settlements of Singapore, Malacca and Penang *(see feature box, below)*.

Highlights

Peranakan life and heritage are thematically presented in 10 permanent galleries. Themes include the origins of the Peranakans, the fastidious 12-day Peranakan wedding, the role of the *nonya*, the Peranakan woman, as well as Peranakan cuisine, which is a major preoccupation in the culture.

Two notable exhibits are located in the **Wedding Gallery**. A 19th-century silk bridal gown, adorned with embroidered phoenixes and peonies, is typical of that worn by Peranakan brides in Singapore and Malacca. Another major exhibit is the wedding bed, ornately carved with auspicious motifs and decorated with embroidered hangings and beads. The wedding bed is traditionally one of the largest pieces of furniture in the homes of wealthy Peranakans.

The **Food and Feasting Gallery** presents glimpses into the unique Peranakan cuisine and dining customs. Elaborately set up here is a *tok panjang* (long table), laden with colourful porcelain of all shapes and sizes, used for the traditional 12-course feast held during weddings and special occasions. Other ceramics on display include the brilliant China-made *kamcheng*. Ranging from a few centimetres to half a metre in diameter, these lidded pots are used for serving food and water.

Peranakans

Peranakan men are known as *baba* and the women *nonya*. They were the first locals to speak English and adopt Western customs during the colonial times. In fact their loyalty to the British led some to describe them as the 'King's Chinese'. They speak a Chinese-Malay patois, and their culture is derived from the traditions of these ethnic groups. Most perceptibly Peranakan culinary heritage is a blend of Malay and Chinese cooking styles and ingredients. Many Peranakan families used to reside in Emerald Hill *(see p.58)* and Katong *(see p.84)* in terrace houses that sport a distinctive architectural style. Having intermarried with other races, Peranakans are becoming less distinct as a racial group.

THE SUBSTATION

Leave the museum and walk down Armenian Street. At no. 45 is **The Substation** ❹ (tel: 6337 7535; www.substation.org), an independent arts centre converted from a disused power station. Its small theatre is often the stage for experimental drama and dance productions. Peep into the gallery; there may be an ongoing exhibition of an emerging visual artist.

NATIONAL MUSEUM

At the end of Armenian Street, cross the road to Stamford Road and turn left after the Singapore Management University's School of Accountancy on your left. Further ahead on the left is the **National Museum ❺** (tel: 6332 3659; www.nationalmuseum.sg; Singapore History Gallery daily 10am–6pm; Singapore Living Galleries daily 10am–8pm; charge; free daily 6pm –8pm). Before you tour the museum, have lunch at **Novus**, see ⑪②.

Restoration

Opened in 1887, the original building was designed by J.F. McNair as the former Raffles Library and Museum. Designed in elegant neo-Palladian style, the building was expanded in 1906, 1914 and 1916. The museum emerged from another major facelift, the most extensive reconstruction and conservation project in its history, in late 2006.

The building, now restored to its former splendour, has a new glass-and-steel wing, whose star attraction is the beautiful **Glass Rotunda**. Designed as a modern interpretation of the original **Rotunda Dome**, the glass rotunda lights up like a lantern at night, with projected images that depict Singapore's history.

For the original Rotunda Dome's restoration, experts took down its curved stained-glass panels, which were then restored by a professional stained-glass artist who used 18th-century reinforcement techniques.

The Victorian floral and square patterns remain as vivid as ever after the stained-glass pieces were buffed and cleaned. Go up on the four-storey **Glass Passage** to view the dome's exterior architectural details such as elegant Palladian motifs and 19th-century fish-scale zinc tiles.

Galleries

There are two main sections in the National Museum: the **History Gallery** and four **Living Galleries**.

The history section traces Singapore's past from the 14th century to the present day through two complementary 'paths' that chronicle key events and everyday experiences of citizens.

The Living Galleries afford insights into everyday life in modern Singapore through its engaging fashion, film, food and photography sections. In the **Food Gallery**, for example, you can find out more about Singapore's street food from the 1950s to 1970s: Not only do you see and 'hear' the installations, you can also catch whiffs of the different types of food and spices.

The **Exhibition Galleries** are where temporary exhibits are staged. A

Food and Drink

② NOVUS CAFÉ, BAR & COURTYARD
National Museum; www.novus.sg; café: 01-04, tel: 6337 1397, daily 10am–6pm; bar and courtyard: 02-04, Mon–Thur 5pm–midnight, Fri–Sat until 1am; $$$$
While you wait for your order of sandwiches, quiches, cakes or milkshakes at the café, browse through the huge collection of design books. Or if you fancy a drink, prop at the 4m (14-ft)-long bar in the posh interior or sit outside in the lovely courtyard, where you can also enjoy live jazz.

prominent past exhibition featured 130 classical Greek and Hellenistic artefacts from the Louvre in Paris.

NATIONAL TREASURES

Don't forget to look out for the 11 National Treasures. These historically significant and rare artefacts, selected from the National Museum's collection, date from the 14th century to the mid-20th century.

Singapore Stone

An important relic of the country's pre-colonial history is the **Singapore Stone**, located in the Singapore History Gallery. It is engraved with the earliest inscription found on the island. What you can see in the museum is the remains of a large boulder that originally stood by the Singapore River, near where the Fullerton Hotel *(see p.40)* stands now.

The boulder split into three parts after it was blown up in the 19th century for the widening of the river. The full inscription, dating from the 10th to the 14th century, has not been deciphered as scholars cannot agree on the date of origin and the language, which

Above: National Treasures – the Singapore Stone, Munshi Abdullah's will and Xin Sai Le puppet stage.

has however been speculated to be a variant of an old Sumatran script.

Munshi's Will

Another highlight in the History Gallery is the 19th-century **will of Munshi Abdullah**, who is known as the Father of modern Malay literature. A contemporary of Stamford Raffles and Colonel William Farquhar, he is most well known for his magnum opus *Hikayat Abdullah* (*The Story of Abdullah*), which contains his firsthand impressions of the island after 1819, the year Sultan Hussein of Johor allowed the British East India Company to establish a trading post in Singapore. Munshi's will, dating to 1854, is a rare document, as wills were uncommon during his time.

Xin Sai Le Puppet Stage

The museum has an excellent Chinese puppetry collection, of which the **Xin Sai Le Puppet Stage**, found in the Film and Wayang Gallery, is another interesting National Treasure. Chinese puppet shows were a popular form of street entertainment for immigrants from the 19th to the early 20th century. This glove-puppet theatre stage, with 1,000 light bulbs, belonged to the Xin Sai Le troupe from the Fujian province in South China, which visited Singapore in the 1930s. The whole theatre could be dismantled or assembled within an hour by the troupe. The collection comes with 45 puppets, 96 costumes, 56 hats, 24 pieces of backdrops, accessories and 20 pieces of props, stored in two wooden chests.

Food and Drink 🍴

③ DOME CAFÉ
01-01 Singapore Art Museum; tel: 6339 0792; daily 10am–10.30pm; $$
Seats outside offer views of the museum's quaint courtyard with fountains. On the menu are cakes, pastries, tarts and gelati.

SINGAPORE ART MUSEUM

From the National Museum, cross Stamford Road to Bencoolen Street, walk past the buildings of the Singapore Management University and turn right. Further along on Bras Basah Road is the **Singapore Art Museum** ➏ (tel: 6332 3222; www.singart.com; daily 10am–7pm, Fri until 9pm; charge).

Historical Building

Hailed as a national monument, the 1855 museum building once housed the St Joseph's Institution, a Catholic boys' school founded in 1852 and run by the La Salle Brothers. After 135 years on Bras Basah Road, the school was relocated in 1987 and the building was sensitively restored as Singapore's national art museum. Note the former chapel, now the museum's auditorium, featuring a stained-glass installation by Filipino contemporary artist Ramon Orlina. Original architectural features that have been retained include the pretty courtyards, shuttered windows and ceramic floor tiles.

Collection

Institutional and private collectors in Singapore avidly amass art from the region, and this museum is one of them. It has an excellent sampling of works by leading Asian artists, such as Affandi and Hendra Gunawan from Indonesia and Chinese Nobel Prize laureate Gao Xingjian.

The museum also holds the Singapore's national art collection. The permanent collection of over 7,500 artworks includes representative works of well-known local artists such as Liu Kang and Georgette Chen. One highlight is Chen's *Still Life with Orange and Apples*. The museum has acquired 94 of her paintings, which comprise portraits, still lifes and landscapes.

The museum's café, **Dome**, see ⑪③, is good for afternoon tea.

Above from far left: Chinese puppets in the National Museum; contemporary art in the Singapore Art Museum.

Above: Georgette Chen's paintings – *Self-Portrait* and *Still Life with Orange and Apples*. **Below:** gallery in the art museum.

MARINA BAY

Iconic structures such as the Marina Bay Sands, the Esplanade Theatres and the Singapore Flyer dominate the Marina Bay district. The area is also considered the city's new downtown with the development of the Marina Bay Financial Centre.

DISTANCE 3km
TIME Full day
START Esplanade
END Helix Bridge
POINTS TO NOTE

Take the MRT to the City Hall station and turn right into CityLink Mall after the fare gates. Follow the signs to Esplanade. From there, explore the entire Marina Bay loop, ending at the Helix Bridge.

Suntec City

Suntec City is home to the Singapore International Convention and Exhibition Centre and the Suntec City Mall (www.suntec city.com. sg). Designed according to feng shui (geomancy) principles, it is modelled after the human hand, with its four tower blocks representing the fingers and the shorter convention centre, the thumb. Held in the 'palm' is the ring-shaped Fountain of Wealth, the largest of its kind in the world.

The Singapore River empties into the Marina Bay, an artificial inlet formed by reclaimed land. Marina Bay is also the name of the area around the bay, the city's new downtown. A landscaped promenade forms a continuous pedestrian route along the waterfront, linking the Esplanade to Collyer Quay and the Marina Bay Sands Integrated Resort.

THE ESPLANADE

Start your tour at **The Esplanade – Theatres on the Bay ❶**. Like many of the world's structures of groundbreaking design (think Eiffel Tower), the S$600 million Esplanade (tel: 6828 8377; www.esplanade.com), which was conceived by British architect Michael Wilford and Singapore's DP Architects, has been a subject of impassioned debate since it was completed in 2002. The spiny exterior of its two colossal domeshaped auditoriums, comprising sharp-edged metal sunshades, have often been compared to the thorny husks of the durian fruit. Singaporeans have, however, grown to love the bold architecture.

Arts Hub

If time permits during your visit, make sure to catch a performance at the Esplanade. Its 1,600-seat concert hall and 2,000-seat theatre have outstanding acoustics. The well-regarded **Singapore Symphony Orchestra** performs its season at the concert hall; tickets are available at the box office (daily noon–8.30pm). The centre hosts musicians and theatre groups all year round.

Food and Drink 🍴

① **SPACE @ MY HUMBLE HOUSE**

02-25 Esplanade Mall; tel: 6423 1881; www.tunglok.com; daily 11.45am–3pm and 6–10.30pm; $$
This casual outlet adjacent to the fine dining My Humble House serves Chinese-style comfort food such as the special Mama Leong chicken rice. A pre-show menu is available for theatre-goers.

Meal Options

After your Esplanade tour, have early lunch at **Space @ My Humble House**, see ⑪①, at the Esplanade Mall. If you return here for an evening performance, try hawker fare at the **Makansutra Gluttons Bay** outside the mall.

ESPLANADE PARK

From the mall, exit onto the **Marina Bay Promenade**. Walk along the waterfront; the view of the CBD skyline from here is fantastic. Continue under the **Esplanade Bridge** to the **Esplanade Park ❷**, a green belt along Connaught Drive.

At the park's northern end is the Victorian-style **Tan Kim Seng Fountain**, constructed to mark the merchant's contribution in 1857 to build the town's water works. The **Cenotaph**, whose granite surface is engraved with the words 'Our Glorious Dead', is dedicated to the 124 British men who lost their lives in World War I. After World War II, more inscriptions were added on the other side of the stone. At the southern end is the **Lim Bo Seng Memorial**, dedicated to the war hero who led the anti-Japanese resistance movement, Force 136, during World War II.

Esplanade Tours

The Esplanade offers guided tours (charge) for groups of at least 20 persons, on which the performing venues, such as the concert hall and the theatre, are visited. If you are on your own, you can opt for the self-guided iTour (tel: 6828 8377; daily 10am–6pm; charge) with a Personal Digital Assistant (PDA). The iTour gives you insights on the public spaces and architecture of The Esplanade and the acoustics features of the performing venues, although you won't be able to access the venues on your own.

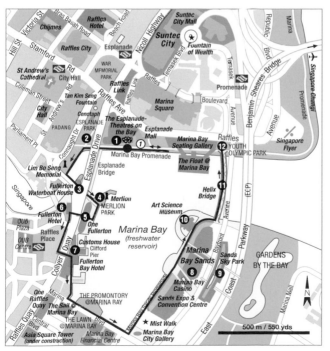

WATERBOAT HOUSE

Head onto the pedestrian path along Anderson Bridge. Ahead is the Art Deco-style **Fullerton Waterboat House ❸** (1919), so named because it supplied water to ships anchored out at sea. Restored with its original curved facade intact, the building now houses a wine bar and Le Saint Julien, a superb French restaurant *(see p.117)*.

MERLION PARK

Just before the Waterboat House, turn left and follow the path to the **Merlion Park ❹**. By the water's edge is a 8.6m (28-ft) -high statue of the water-spewing Merlion. First unveiled in 1964, the tourism icon has a lion's head, which recalls the myth of ancient Singapore's founder Sang Nila Utama, said to have spotted a lion on the island *c.*14th century. Its fish tail symbolises the city's beginnings as a fishing village.

FULLERTON BUILDINGS

Next to the Merlion Park is the glass-and-steel **One Fullerton ❺**, with a clutch of restaurants and cafés offering alfresco, waterfront seating.

The **Fullerton Hotel ❻** is linked by an underpass to One Fullerton. It occupies a 1924 building named after Robert Fullerton, the first governor of the Straits Settlements, and a fine example of the Edwardian Baroque neoclassical style that once dominated the Civic District. Before it was restored and reopened as a hotel in 2001, the building was the heart of social and commercial life as the Chamber of Commerce and the General Post Office.

COLLYER QUAY

The Fullerton Waterboat House, Fullerton Hotel and One Fullerton

---

The Singapore Flyer

On the same side of the bayfront as the Esplanade is the 165m (540-ft) -high Singapore Flyer (tel: 6333 3311; www.singapore flyer.com; daily 8.30am–10.30pm; charge). When it opened in 2008 it displaced the London Eye as the world's highest observation wheel. Unobstructed in all directions, the giant wheel offers panoramic views of Malaysian and Indonesian islands as well as Singapore's city skyline, which is particularly scintillating at night.

make up a leisure precinct known as **Fullerton Heritage**, which also comprises the **Collyer Quay** area, further south along the waterfront. Collyer Quay once bustled with clipper ships and lighters before the activities moved to Keppel Harbour. The re-developed **Customs House** ❼ today houses The Fullerton Bay Hotel, several restaurants and bars with a stunning view of the bay. From Customs House, walk along waterfront promenade which links to **Marina Bay Sands** ❽, an integrated resort which has transformed Singapore's skyline since it was completed in 2010.

MARINA BAY SANDS

The reclaimed Marina Bay area bordering the waterfront is a scintillating focal point on this island. To the west of Marina Bay Sands Integrated Resort is the **Marina Bay Financial Centre**, an extension of the CBD. Besides housing banks and offices, within the vicinity is The Sail residential apartment.

The centrepiece of this area is the massive **Marina Bay Sands** (www.marinabaysands.com) – the most expensive ever built by the American casino-resort giant Las Vegas Sands. This mega leisure, entertainment and hospitality complex features a casino, luxury hotel, convention facilities, high-end boutiques, a theatre, and restaurants. You can stop for a meal at one of the many eateries ranging from local food to restaurants by some of the world's finest celebrity chefs.

One of the many "engineering wonders" here is the 200-m **Sands Sky Park** ❾, a fascinating structure designed by architect Moshe Safdie. Perched on top of the three lofty hotel towers are a sweeping 1.2 hectare tropical park with landscaped gardens, an observation deck, and an infinity pool with amazing views of the skyline.

Across the highway via a pedestrian bridge is an area called Gardens by the Bay (www.gardensbythebay.org.sg) featuring conservatories and lush waterfront gardens. Adjacent to Marina Bay Sands complex is the **Art Science Museum** ❿ (tel: 6688 8826; open daily 10am-10pm; charge). The unique white coloured lotus-shaped building houses galleries exhibiting art, science, media, technology, design and architecture. If you have time, spend a couple of hours here exploring the different visiting and permanent exhibitions in the world of art and science.

Another engineering masterpiece nearby is the world's first **double helix curved bridge** ⓫ which allows pedestrians to walk across from Marina Bay Sands to the other side of the waterfront where luxury hotels like Ritz-Carlton Millenia and Mandarin Oriental are located. This bridge with its look-out points affords beautiful sunsets and views of the bay. You can end your tour at the **Youth Olympic Park** ⓬, an 'art park' with creative installations by local youth. It is right at the end of the Helix Bridge and near the Floating Stadium. Alternatively, walk over to the foot of the Singapore Flyer and have a meal at the 1960s themed food street.

Above from far left:
Merlion Park;
Fullerton Hotel;
looking across the
bay.

Night Racing
The Formula 1 Singapore Grand Prix, held in September each year, is the first and only night-time race in F1's history. It takes place on over 5km (3 miles) of public roads in the Marina Bay area. The pit building is located next to the Singapore Flyer. See www.singaporegp.sg for details.

SINGAPORE RIVER

The Singapore River is where the city's modern history began. Take a trip along the river down memory lane, to see colonial-era bridges, stately buildings and conservation shophouses that reflect the city's past.

Old Bridges
The Singapore River flows under 12 bridges, many of which are historical structures with beautiful designs.

Above from left: bumboats on the Singapore River; Cavenagh Bridge and the Fullerton Hotel.

DISTANCE 1.5km (1 mile)
TIME 3–4 hours
START Merlion Park
END Clarke Quay
or Merlion Park
POINTS TO NOTE
Walk from the Raffles Place MRT station to the Merlion Park or take a taxi to One Fullerton, which is next to the park. This is recommended as an afternoon-to-evening tour. You can combine this tour with walk 3 (see p.38).

Spanning almost 4km (2½ miles) from its mouth at Marina Bay to Kim Seng Bridge on the other end, the Singapore River was the island's commercial lifeline for more than a century. It was where Stamford Raffles, founder of modern Singapore, and early immigrants first landed. The swamps and floating skulls deposited by pirates are long gone, as are the coolies, junks and warehouses. Its quays are now lined by colourful conservation shophouses and warehouses, and its surroundings speckled with colonial-era buildings.

River Cruise

A leisurely way to enjoy the sights along the banks is to board the **Singapore River Experience** (tel: 63366111; www.rivercruise.com.sg), a pleasant 30-minute cruise on an environmentally friendly electric bumboat, designed to look like a traditional one of yesteryear. Purchase your ticket (daily 9am–11pm) at the Singapore River Cruises & Leisure booth at the jetty at the **Merlion Park ❶**. The boat wends its way from Marina Bay *(see*

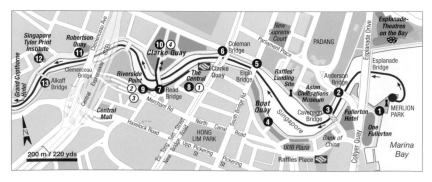

p.38) to Boat Quay and Clarke Quay, passing under several bridges, and then turns around at the Liang Court jetty for the return journey to the Merlion Park. If you have more time, you can also opt for the 45-minute cruise further upriver to Robertson Quay.

However, if you prefer to alight at any point along the river, such as at Clarke Quay as recommended in this tour, purchase a one-way river taxi ticket *(see margin)*.

HISTORICAL BRIDGES

When you board the boat, be sure to take advantage of the good photo opportunities of buildings like The Esplanade – Theatres on the Bay *(see p.38)* and Fullerton Hotel *(see p.40)*.

The cruise takes you under the first bridge, **Anderson Bridge ❷**, built in 1910 to link the colonial district (now the Civic District) and the commercial district (present-day Raffles Place).

You then pass under **Cavenagh Bridge ❸**. Made in Scotland and reassembled in Singapore, the bridge was named after Major-General Orfeur Cavenagh, Governor of the Straits Settlement from 1859 to 1867. It was originally planned as a drawbridge but upon completion was found to be appropriate only as a fixed structure. Now it serves a pedestrian bridge linking the north and south banks.

BOAT QUAY

After Cavenagh Bridge is **Raffles' Landing Site** *(see p.28)* and the **Asian Civilisations Museum** *(see p.28)* to your right. You can also see the sci-fi-inspired disc of the **New Supreme Court** *(see p.27)*.

As the cruise continues, to your left is **Boat Quay ❹**, which runs along the south bank between Cavenagh Bridge and Elgin Bridge.

Boat Quay was a trading hub from the colonial days until the 1970s when lighters were banned from the river, and flotsam and jetsam was cleared. Its shophouses, which held cargo in the early days, were restored to their former glory and updated as restaurants and bars.

Today's Boat Quay has seen better days, having been eclipsed by the

Water Taxi
The operator of the Singapore River Experience cruise also runs a river taxi service that takes you from one point to another along the Singapore River. Rates depend on destinations. Let the attendants know in advance where you want to disembark. Buy your ticket and board at any of the nine jetties along the Singapore River.

The Belly of the Carp

Many Chinese believe that health, wealth, relationships and success or failure in career and business are all governed by *feng shui* (geomancy). Seen from above, Boat Quay curves like the belly of a carp, which Chinese consider to be an auspicious creature. In the early days Boat Quay's propitious shape attracted Chinese businessmen, who believed that the area emanated good energy. It is also no surprise that many banks have flourished here, because at this strategic point, the river swells into a large body of water, hence symbolising the growth of wealth

Above from left:
Penny Black pub;
Alkaff Bridge.

Watering Holes
Avoid the dodgy end of Boat Quay, filled with karaoke bars. Recommended spots nearer to Raffles Place are Penny Black Victorian London Pub (tel: 6538 2300; www. pennyblack.com.sg; Mon–Thur 11.30am–1am, Fri–Sat until 2am, Sun until midnight) and Harry's Bar (tel: 6538 3029; www.harrys. com.sg; Sun–Thur 11am–1am, Fri–Sat until 2am), with live jazz. egulars are mainly bankers and brokers from Raffles Place.

Below:
Riverside Point.

revitalised Clarke Quay *(see below)*. Nevertheless, its eclectic mix of alfresco eateries, lively Irish pubs and trendy bars still appeals to executives from the vicinity and tourists seeking to dine or drink by the river.

MORE BRIDGES

At the end of Boat Quay is **Elgin Bridge 5**, named after the governor-general of India from 1862 to 1863, Lord James Bruce Elgin. The current concrete structure was completed in 1929 and replaced an earlier iron one brought in from India in 1862. The bridge was constructed as a link between the Chinese on the south side of the river and the Indian merchants of High Street on the north.

The cruise then passes under the concrete **Coleman Bridge 6**. Its appearance today is a far cry from the original Palladian-style brick bridge designed by Irish architect George Coleman and built in 1840. The present concrete bridge opened in 1986 to better cope with heavy traffic flow.

The next bridge is **Read Bridge 7**, built in 1889 and named after businessman and legislator William Henry Read. In the early days Chinese storytellers entertained Chinese coolies with classic tales of history and chivalry on this bridge.

RIVERSIDE POINT

If you have bought a river taxi ticket, alight at the Riverside Point jetty. A short walk away is **The Central 8** (tel: 6532 9922; www.thecentral.com. sg; daily 11am–10pm), a Japanese-themed mall with boutiques selling streetwear and accessories. Sip a cup of local tea at **Ya Kun Kaya Toast**, see ①①. Or have a bite and drink at the restaurants at **Riverside Point 9**, such as **Café Iguana**, see ①②, and **Brewerkz**, see ①③. Then, linger around the lively area before crossing Read Bridge to Clarke Quay.

CLARKE QUAY

Clarke Quay 10, spanning five blocks, was named after Lieutenant-General Sir Andrew Clarke, the second governor of the Straits Settlement. Until the 1970s, it hummed with much activity as bumboats carried cargo from ships to the warehouses on its banks.

Wander at will and look a little closer to discover some of its history. At its

southern end, for instance, on the wall of the last shophouse is a sign proclaiming that it was once Whampoa's Ice House. A wealthy Chinese landowner, Whampoa gifted the land where the Singapore Botanic Gardens sits today to the British, who gave him the land at Clarke Quay in return.

Nightlife Hub

Today's Clarke Quay hums to a different beat, with its restored warehouses housing restaurants and notable clubs like Attica *(see p 122)*. The area is pleasant to stroll around in; huge canopies provide cool shade over its lanes in the day and are stunningly lit at night, while lily-pad platforms offer pleasant alfresco dining over the river. If you have not had dinner, consider **The Pump Room**, see 🍴④.

ROBERTSON QUAY

If you have opted for the 45-minute river cruise, your boat will head on to **Robertson Quay** ⑪. In the old days, this part of the riverbank was filled with warehouses. Now it has been mostly taken over by luxury apartments. The 19th-century warehouses that remain have been restored and are occupied by bars and restaurants.

Print Institute

The boat goes past the **Singapore Tyler Print Institute** ⑫ (tel: 6336 3663; www.stpi.com.sg; Tue–Sat 10am–6pm; free), a gallery with interesting print exhibitions, worth a visit if you have the time.

Alkaff Bridge

After the print institute, the boat passes under the pedestrian **Alkaff Bridge** ⑬, named after the wealthy Arab Alkaff family. Completed in 1997, the bridge has been painted by the late Filipino artist Pacita Abad with help from a team of rope specialists, using some 50 different colours and 900 litres of paint.

The boat turns around near the Grand Copthorne Waterfront hotel and then makes its way back to the Merlion Park.

HiPPO Cruise

Another boat cruise on the Singapore River is the 25-minute HiPPO River Cruise (tel: 6338 6077, www.ducktours.com.sg; daily 9am–10pm), which begins and ends at Clarke Quay. A guide onboard offers live commentary on the sights along the river.

Food and Drink

① YA KUN KAYA TOAST
The Central #01-31; Tel: 6534 7332;daily 7.30am – 10.30pm; $
Have a cup of local tea or coffee at this outlet. If you are feeling peckish, order a crispy stack of kaya toast (toast with coconut jam).

② CAFÉ IGUANA
01-03 Riverside Point; tel: 6236 1275; www.cafeiguana.com; Mon–Thur 4pm–1am, Fri until 3am, Sat noon–3am, Sun noon–1am; $$
This lively restaurant is always packed, thanks to its delicious quesadillas, tortillas and salsas, and cheap margaritas during Happy Hour. It also offers over 150 types of Webber blue agave tequila.

③ BREWERKZ
01-05/06 Riverside Point; tel: 6438 7438; www.brewerkz.com; Sun–Thurs noon–midnight, Fri–Sat until 1am; $$$
This microbrewery-restaurant produces over 2,500 hectolitres of handcrafted beer annually. American-style dishes from the Deep South, the Southwest and California are served.

④ THE PUMP ROOM
01-09/10 The Foundry, Clarke Quay; tel: 6334 2628; www.pumproomasia.com; Mon–Sat noon–3am, Sun 10.30am–3am; $$$
The contemporary Australian specialities at this microbrewery and bistro include Thai-style beef salad, steak and kidney pie cooked with dark beer, and sticky date pudding with toffee anglaise. Also try the freshly brewed speciality beers.

5

CENTRAL BUSINESS DISTRICT

The modern and the traditional collide and coalesce in the financial district. On this walk, gaze at gleaming skyscrapers, admire quirky sculptures, view feng shui-friendly architectural features, and visit age-old places of worship.

Above from left:
the CBD; incense
coils at the Wak Hai
Cheng Temple.

DISTANCE 2.5km (1½ miles)
TIME Half a day
START Raffles Place
END red dot design museum
POINT TO NOTE
Start your tour after 9.30pm or 2pm
to avoid the crowds.

Public Art

Peppered around the CBD are a handful of sculptures. Close to the riverside entrance of Raffles Place is Taiwanese sculptor Yang Ying-Feng's monumental *Progress and Advancement*, a celebration of the city's commercial life commissioned by the late banker Lien Ying Chow. At the ground-floor atrium of UOB Plaza is Salvador Dali's bronze *Homage to Newton*. Just outside the atrium is the voluptuous bronze *Bird*, by Columbian artist Fernando Botero, which was inspired by the dove, the universal symbol of peace. Ouside OCBC Centre is British sculptor Henry Moore's *Reclining Figure*. When it was first installed, it suffered from corrosion caused by the humid climate, and was subsequently treated to acquire the golden hue it wears today. There are also other bronze sculptures, which depict life in the early days, along the Singapore River.

The Central Business District runs close to the Marina Bay waterfront from the Singapore River to Keppel Road. Soaring towers of finance and business line its main arterials of Shenton Way, Robinson Road, Anson Road, Cecil Street and Battery Road. The tallest buildings are centred around **Raffles Place ❶**, a buzzing open-air plaza with the Raffles Place MRT station underground.

Background

In the early days Raffles Place was known as Commercial Square, originally conceived by Stamford Raffles as part of his 1822 town plan. Grand structures housing banks and offices stood here, overlooking a landscaped centre with trees and flower beds. Also an important shopping destination for upper-crust society, Commercial Square was where Singapore's first department store, Robinsons, was founded in 1858. Destroyed in a fire in 1972, it now has branches in Orchard Road *(see p.59)* and Raffles City *(see p.26)*.

SKYSCRAPERS

Surrounding Raffles Place are a few notable skyscrapers, all measuring

280m (920ft) tall, which is the maximum height allowed by the aviation authorities: OUB Centre, Republic Plaza and UOB Plaza.

Japanese architect Kisho Kurokawa designed the dark, glazed **Republic Plaza ❷**, at the end of D'Almeida Street. This tapering tower won him the World Best Architecture Award from FIABCI in 1997.

From Raffles Place turn left onto Chulia Street. The twin towers of **UOB Plaza ❸**, one of the most recognised icons of the city skyline, are designed by another Japanese architect, Kenzo Tange. He fused his vision with that of Lim Chong Keat, his counterpart for the original octagonal 38-storey UOB Building, adding more levels that are turned at 45 degrees relative to one another, to give the building a unique chiselled look.

OCBC Centre

Continue on Chulia Street to South Canal Road. You will reach **OCBC Centre ❹**, designed by I.M. Pei. This 52-storey, the first foreigner-designed skyscraper after independence, was completed in 1976. Nicknamed 'the Calculator', it has three distinctive tiers

separating windows that resemble button pads. Henry Moore's *Reclining Figure (see feature box, p.46)* stands in front of OCBC Centre.

Lunch Option

Opposite OCBC Centre is Boat Quay *(see p.43)*. On Circular Road is **Molly Malone's**, see ⑪①, good for pub grub.

WAK HAI CHENG TEMPLE

After lunch, backtrack on South Canal Road and continue on Philip Street. At the corner with Church Street is

Above: lantern at the Wak Hai Cheng Temple.

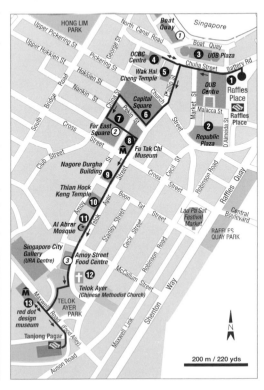

Food and Drink 🍴

① **MOLLY MALONE'S**
56 Circular Road; tel: 6536 2029; www.molly-malone.com; Sun–Mon 11am–midnight, Tues–Sat 11am – 2am; $$
At this Irish pub, enjoy excellent pub grub, such as fish and chips, shepherd's pie and Irish lamb stew.

the **Wak Hai Cheng Temple ⑤** (tel: 6533 8537; daily 7am–5.30pm), built in the 1850s by the Teochew community for the protection of traders travelling between Singapore and China. A constellation of deities, including Ma Chu Po, the Goddess of the Sea, and the Eight Immortals, are enshrined here. Suspended in the forecourt are large coils of incense, which can take up to 10 days to burn.

Cross Church Street to **Capital Square ⑥**, an office block with a feature of cascading water, presumably installed to invite prosperity, for in Chinese belief, water is wealth.

FAR EAST SQUARE

Take the path between Capital Square and China Street. Ahead is **Ya Kun**, see ⑪②, an institution for *kaya* (coconut

jam) toast. Enter **Far East Square ⑦** by the Metal Gate, one of the complex's five gates, each representing an element of the Chinese universe: metal, wood, water, fire and earth.

Far East Square is a conservation area of restored shophouses in four architectural styles prevalent from 1840s to 1960s – Early, First Transitional, Late and Second Transitional *(see feature box, p.49).* Bounded by Cross, Telok Ayer and China streets, the complex houses mainly offices and restaurants.

FU TAK CHI MUSEUM

Follow the signs, through a glass door, to the **Fu Tak Chi Museum ⑧** (tel: 6532 7868; daily 10am–10pm; free), formerly a Taoist temple set up by Hakka and Cantonese immigrants in 1824. It displays artefacts donated by early Chinatown residents.

TELOK AYER STREET

From the museum, turn right on Telok Ayer Street. Meaning 'water bay' in Malay, this street once stood by the shore. Its shophouses are mainly of the First Transitional style, with narrow fronts and modest ornamentation.

Nagore Durgha Building

At the corner with Boon Tat Street is the **Nagore Durgha Building ⑨**, built in the late 1820s by Tamil Muslims as a meeting place and house of worship. With its intricate minarets, arches and niches, it has been described as a multilayered wedding cake.

> ## Food and Drink 🍴
>
> **② YA KUN**
> 01-01 Far East Square; tel: 6438 3638; www.yakun.com; Mon–Fri 7.30am–6.30pm, Sat–Sun 8.30am–5pm; $
> Established in 1944, Yakun serves a unique Singapore-style breakfast or teatime snack of soft-boiled eggs and *kaya* toast (grilled bread with coconut jam and butter).
>
> **③ AMOY STREET FOOD CENTRE**
> Corner of Telok Ayer and Amoy streets; $
> Great for local fare such as minced-meat noodles (noodles tossed with a chilli-vinegar sauce and topped with minced pork) and *char kway teow* (fried rice noodles with cockles).

Thian Hock Keng Temple

The next place of worship is the **Thian Hock Keng Temple** ⓾, the Temple of Heavenly Happiness (tel: 6423 4616; daily 7.30am–5.30pm; www.thianhock keng.com.sg). Hokkien immigrants set up a joss house in the 1820s in gratitude to Ma Chu Po for their safe arrival. This became the Thian Hock Keng, built in 1842 without one single nail. Dragons, venerated for protection on sea voyages, adorn the roofs and pillars.

Al Abrar Mosque

The **Al Abrar Mosque** ⓫ (tel: 6220 6306; daily 5–7am and 11.30am–9pm) is a few doors down. Built in the mid-1850s by the Indian Chulia community, it replaced the thatched hut that was established on the same site in 1827.

Further along is the **Amoy Street Food Centre**, see ⓶⓷.

Telok Ayer Methodist Church

Follow the curve of the road. The 1925 **Telok Ayer Chinese Methodist**

Church ⓬ (tel: 6324 4001; Mon–Fri 9am–5pm, Sat until 1pm; www.tacmc. org.sg), on your left, combines Chinese and Western elements such as Art Deco windows and European-style columns.

RED DOT MUSEUM

Go through the Telok Ayer Park and cross Maxwell Road to the **red dot Traffic** building. Built in 1928, it housed the Traffic Police headquarters before it was refurbished and painted a striking red. It is now occupied by advertising agencies, a few bars, a café and the **red dot design museum** ⓭ (tel: 6327 8027; www.red-dot.sg; Mon–Tue, Fri 11am–6pm, Sat–Sun until 8pm; charge). Run by the German body that presents the prestigious red dot design awards, the museum has exhibitions of slick product designs from around the world.

Exit the museum and turn right on Maxwell Road. The underground Tanjong Pagar MRT station is on the right after Wallich Street.

Art Market
Worth checking out at red dot Traffic is MAAD (Market of Artists & Designers; tel: 6534 7209; www.maad.sg; 1st weekend of every month 11am–8pm), a unique, curated bazaar showcasing only original jewellery, home accessories and artworks by local emerging artists and designers.

Shophouses

Singapore's downtown shophouses, so called because their ground floor was used for business and the upper levels were residences, feature an architectural style known as Chinese Baroque or Singapore Eclectic. Initiated by Raffles, the style reflects Malay, Chinese and European influences. Each row of houses, built of masonry with tile roofs, is fronted by a covered path called the 'five-foot way', which is exactly five foot wide. The style was later adopted for residential terrace houses. Over the years, five distinct styles developed: Early, First Transitional, Late, Second Transitional and Art Deco. Many of the shophouses have been restored to their original splendour.

CHINATOWN

Like the city's other ethnic enclaves, Chinatown appeals with its fascinating blend of cultures. Visit a mosque, Hindu shrine and Buddhist temple, and explore its narrow streets, traditional shops and market stalls.

DISTANCE 1.5km (1 mile)
TIME Half a day
START Jamae Mosque
END Singapore City Gallery
POINTS TO NOTE
Take a taxi to Jamae Mosque at the corner of Mosque Street and South Bridge Road. Alternatively, take the MRT to the Chinatown station. The mosque is a short walk away.

Above from left: Chinese trinkets; roof details of the Sri Mariamman Temple.

TCM Shop
Across South Bridge Road from Sri Mariamman Temple is Eu Yan Sang, a traditional Chinese medicine business that dates back to 1879. 'Eu' is the name of the family that founded it, and 'Yan Sang' means 'caring for mankind' in Cantonese. The shop stocks over 1,000 types of Chinese herbs and medicinal products, some of which, like herbal candies and bottle bird's-nest soup, make interesting souvenirs.

It seems odd that this city, with a majority Chinese population, has a Chinatown. The neighbourhood only came to be known by this name as a result of the tourism board's efforts to promote the city's ethnic enclaves, although it has existed since the early days, when Chinese immigrants congregated south of the Singapore River.

Today's Chinatown is hemmed in by the soaring high-rises of the CBD, but vestiges of the traditional can still be seen. Conservation shophouses hold decades-old businesses, which stand shoulder to shoulder with even older places of worship. Medical halls dispense herbal cures, and exotic sights and smells, from rare Asian ingredients in the fresh-produce market to the pungent aroma of the durian fruit, still dominate the area.

JAMAE MOSQUE

Chinatown has its share of Chinese temples, but it also has some of the most well-known places of worship of other faiths. This walk starts on South Bridge Road at the **Jamae Mosque** ❶ (tel: 6221 4165; daily 9.30am–6pm). Built in 1826 by Tamil Muslims, it sports an eclectic mix of architectural styles, with pagoda-like minarets, a South India-style entrance gate and neoclassical prayer halls.

SRI MARIAMMAN TEMPLE

Cross Pagoda Street to the **Sri Mariamman Temple** ❷ (tel: 6223 4064; daily 7am–noon and 6–9pm). The temple was built in 1827 by Naraina Pillai, who accompanied Raffles on his second visit to Singapore in 1819. Dedicated to the goddess Mariamman, known for curing serious illnesses, it has

Food and Drink
① TOGI
11 Mosque Street; tel: 6221 0830; Mon – Sat noon-2pm, 6pm-9pm; $$ Located in a narrow shophouse, Togi serves homey Korean fare including comforting chicken ginseng soup, spicy tofu seafood soup, steamboat (hotpot) as well as other Korean favourites.

a *gopuram* (tower), adorned with vivid renditions of Hindu deities, at the entrance. If you happen to be here on the holy days of Tuesday and Friday, you can see brightly clad devotees offering *puja* (prayers) under the watchful eyes of the images on the colourful ceiling frescoes. This temple is the site of the celebrations for Theemithi, the annual fire-walking festival that takes place around October or November, during which devotees tread on white-hot embers in a state of trance.

CHINATOWN HERITAGE CENTRE

Walk down **Pagoda Street**. Tucked among the many brightly coloured shophouses, at no. 46–50, is the **Chinatown Heritage Centre ❸** (tel: 6221 9556; www.chinatownheritage centre.sg; daily 9am–8pm; charge). Using authentic furniture, utensils and other paraphernalia, the museum brings to life the harsh living conditions of Chinatown residents in the early years.

TRENGGANU STREET

Turn right on New Bridge Road and then right again onto **Mosque Street**.

Togi, see ⑪①, serves great Korean dishes and steamboat (hotpot) which is great for sharing. After your meal, retrace your steps, past Pagoda Street, and turn left onto Temple Street. You then come to the junction with **Trengganu Street ❹**, previously an opera street with theatre stages and brothels, and now a pedestrian mall

with vendors selling souvenirs, handicrafts and paintings.

In the days leading up to Chinese New Year, this whole area teems with stalls selling all manner of festive goodies, cured meats, mandarin oranges and auspicious decorations. It is a must to visit Chinatown one or two weeks before the New Year, if only to experience the joyous buzz.

CHINATOWN COMPLEX

Turn right onto Trengganu Street. At the corner with Smith Street is **Chinatown Complex ❺**. This is perhaps one of the best places to catch glimpses of local life. At its basement,

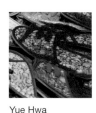

Yue Hwa
The pedestrian bridge extending from Pagoda Street across New Bridge Road and Eu Tong Sen Street leads to Yue Hwa (tel: 6538 4222; www.yuehwa.com. sg; daily 11am–9pm), an emporium for all things Chinese, from embroidered slippers to Chinese herbs.

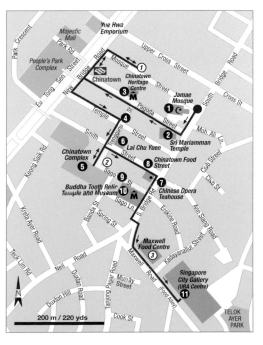

Night Market
Over 200 stalls at the Chinatown Night Market (daily 11am–11pm), sprawling over Pagoda, Trengganu and Sago streets, offer trinkets, tourist souvenirs and traditional Chinese goods like calligraphy and masks.

market vendors sell all manner of fresh produce and dried goods. Upstairs is a food centre with plenty of stalls dishing up excellent, old-fashioned hawker fare. For a Western-style snack, try Austrian-style sausages at **Erich's Wuerstelstand**, see ⑪②, located at the corner of Trengganu and Sago streets.

LAI CHUN YUEN

Diagonally opposite Chinatown Complex on Trengganu Street is **Lai Chun Yuen** ❻, a former Chinese opera house dating back to the 1920s. This is one of the earliest three-storey buildings in the area, with a verandah running around the top level.

SMITH STREET

Further along **Smith Street** is the **Chinese Opera Teahouse** ❼ (no. 5; tel: 6323 4862; www.ctcopera.com.sg; Tue–Sun noon–5pm). Here you can have tea and snacks at traditional Chinese tables, surrounded by displays of opera costumes. On Friday and Saturday from 7pm to 9pm, you can enjoy dinner here while you watch Cantonese opera excerpts (bookings advised).

Chinatown Food Street
Street hawkers have made a comeback at the open-air **Chinatown Food Street** ❽ (daily 5pm–11pm) along Smith Street. Return here in the evening to sample local staples like *char kway teow* (fried flat rice noodles) and fish ball noodles.

SAGO STREET

Walk down Smith Street and turn right on South Bridge Road. A few steps away is **Sago Street** ❾. Named after the numerous sago factories that operated here in the 1840s, the street was also a red-light district in the early 20th century. Today it is a pedestrian-only lane flanked by shophouses housing old-style Chinese medical halls and pastry shops on one side and souvenir and clothing stalls on the other.

BUDDHA TOOTH RELIC TEMPLE

Sandwiched between Sago Street and Sago Lane is the **Buddha Tooth Relic Temple and Museum** ❿ (tel: 6220 0220; www.btrts.org.sg; daily 7am–7pm; free). Its architecture, interiors and

---

Food and Drink 🍴

② ERICH'S WUERSTELSTAND
2&3 Trengganu Street; mobile tel: 9627 4882; daily 3pm–late; $
This stall is run by an Austrian chef who has lived in Asia for almost two decades. His grilled sausages include the traditional bratwurst and the boiled bockwurst served in a crispy roll topped with mustard.

③ MAXWELL FOOD CENTRE
Corner of South Bridge Road and Maxwell Road; daily 7am–10pm; $
This bustling food centre is a great place for dining round the clock from breakfast through to supper. Stalls that often have a queue are Zhen Zhen (no. 54) for its congee and Tian Tian (no. 10) for its chicken rice.

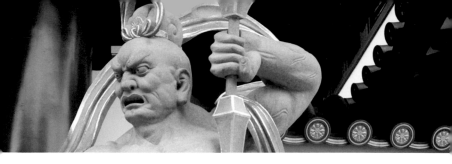

statuary are inspired by the styles of the Tang dynasty – a golden age for Buddhism in China. The temple's centrepiece is one of the Buddha's sacred teeth, an object dogged by much controversy; its authenticity has been doubted by Buddhism scholars and some members of the public. It is held on the fourth floor in a golden stupa and only taken out for viewing on Vesak Day and Chinese New Year. More than half of the 420kg (930lbs) of gold needed to construct the stupa was donated by devotees. The stupa is unveiled for viewing two times a day (9am and 3pm).

Highlights
Entering the 80m (260ft) -high **100 Dragons Hall** on the ground level, you see an intricately carved 5m (20ft) -tall Maitreya Buddha image. A hundred other Buddha statues line both sides of the hall. On the third floor is the climate-controlled **Buddhist Culture Museum** (daily 8am–6pm), with precious Buddha images collected from all over Asia. On the roof you can admire the *Dendrobium Buddha Tooth*, an orchid hybrid named after the temple, and turn the huge prayer wheel in the **Ten Thousand Buddha Pavilion**. Some 10,000 tiny Buddha images are enshrined along the galleries.

SINGAPORE CITY GALLERY

After your temple visit, cross South Bridge Road to the **Maxwell Food Centre**, see ⑪③, for some refreshments before continuing along Maxwell Road to the **Singapore City Gallery ⑪** (tel: 6321 8321; www.ura. gov.sg/gallery; Mon–Sat 9am–5pm; free) at the URA Centre.

The gallery's highlight is an enormous scaled and detailed 11x11m (36x36ft) architectural model of Singapore's central area. Spread over two storeys are the rest of the gallery's 50 exhibits, including a multimedia exhibit that charts Singapore's architectural development over the past 180 years. You can also survey the vision the planners have for this island in the 21st century.

Ann Siang Hill

The narrow Club Street and curvy Ann Siang Hill behind South Bridge Road, are worth a detour. The shophouses here used to be occupied by mainly Chinese clan associations and clubs. A few clubs remain today, continuing to serve a social function for their elderly members who pass their time playing mahjong or enjoying Chinese opera music. The rest of the shophouses have been transformed into trendy bars, restaurants, lifestyle stores such as Style: Nordic (39 Ann Siang Road; tel: 6423 9114; www.stylenordic.com), with Scandinavian furniture and apparel as well as a luxury boutique hotel, The Club Hotel (28 Ann Siang Road; tel: 6808 2188; www.theclub.com.sg) housed in a 1900 heritage building

ORCHARD ROAD

No visit to Singapore is complete without a day's work on its most famous shopping artery, dense with ritzy malls and sidewalk cafés. The strip also has an enclave with exquisite Chinese Baroque–style houses.

DISTANCE 3km (2 miles), not including the distances covered in the malls
TIME A full day
START Tanglin Mall
END MacDonald House
POINTS TO NOTE
To get to Tanglin Mall, at the corner of Tanglin and Grange roads, take a taxi or bus no. 36, which stops in front of The Regent hotel. Most shops and malls open at 10.30 or 11am and close at 9 or 10pm.

Background

Orchard Road was so named because of the many nutmeg, pepper and fruit plantations found here in the 1800s. In the 1840s the area was also dotted with cemeteries. But by the 20th century, Orchard metamorphosed into a vibrant commercial centre and later into the city's flashiest shopping address and style headquarters, teeming with malls and luxury hotels.

The city's passion for shopping is easily demonstrated by the numerous, over-crowded malls on Orchard Road. It would be too exhausting to visit all the malls in a day; this tour guides you to the shopping highlights and a few historical sights, starting from the Tanglin area.

Food and Drink 🍴

① **CAFFE BEVIAMO**
02-K1 Tanglin Mall, 163 Tanglin Road; tel: 6738 7906; daily 9.30am–6.30pm; $$
Generously portioned sandwiches, salads, antipasti and pastas. Order the luscious sticky date pudding sandwich with vanilla ice cream.

TANGLIN ROAD

Begin with a fortifying brunch at **Caffe Beviamo**, see 🍴①, in **Tanglin Mall ❶**, which has boutiques and gourmet-food shops.

Art and Antiques

From Tanglin Mall, walk up Tanglin Road to **Tudor Court ❷**. If you are interested in Asian artefacts and antiques, many shops here are worth a browse. The upscale French gourmet store Hédiard is also here, with caviar, wines, preserves, teas and spices.

Continue past **St Regis Hotel** and on to **Tanglin Shopping Centre ❸**. The latter's dated exterior belies the quality antiques and art found in its galleries and shops.

FORUM AND HILTON

Follow the bend around Orchard Parade Hotel into Orchard Road proper. On the right is **Forum The Shopping Mall ❹**, filled with boutiques for children and mums.

Hilton Hotel

Further on from Forum, look out for the two Chinese warrior statues in front of the **Hilton Hotel ❺**. These 'doorway guardians' are said to offer protection from evil spirits. The hotel's **shopping arcade** is a good stop for designer jewellery and haute couture in the likes of Issey Miyake and Giorgio Armani.

It also connects to the **Four Seasons Hotel**'s **shopping arcade** just behind. The **Club 21** gallery here features Balenciaga, Mulberry, Marc Jacobs and other luxe fashion labels.

Palais Renaissance

Opposite the Hilton is the swanky **Palais Renaissance ❻**, a fashion playground for the well-heeled with the designer boutiques such as DKNY and a Passion Hair Salon frequented by local celebrities.

On the opposite side, after the ageing Far East Shopping Centre, is **Liat Towers ❼**, which hosts Spanish brands Zara and Massimo Dutti as well as luxury label Hermès. Beside it is **Wheelock Place ❽**, designed by Japanese superstar architect Kisho

Above from far left: brand name at Orchard; bustling Orchard Road; Wheelock Place.

Thai Presence
When King Chulalongkorn visited Singapore in the 1890s, he bought the property next to Palais Renaissance. This is today the Thai Embassy. It hosts an annual Thai Festival in its spacious garden in June, during which you can catch a whiff of pungent durians even from a distance. For dates and other information, check www.thaiembassy.sg or call tel: 6737 2158.

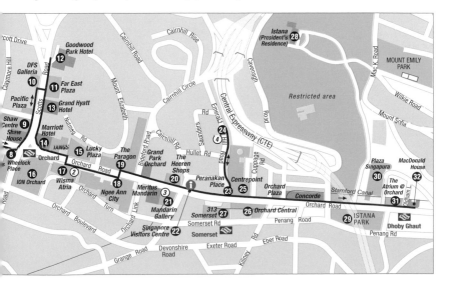

Above from left:
Marriott Hotel; outside the Singapore Visitors Centre; Goodwood Park Hotel.

Night Shopping
On Saturday nights many malls on Orchard Road, such as Wisma Atria and Centrepoint, are open until 11pm.

Below: Wisma Atria.

Kurokawa. Its glass pyramid is a landmark. Found here are Marks & Spencer and a variety of speciality shops and eateries.

SCOTTS ROAD

Cross the road to **Shaw Centre ❾**, home to the Japanese department store Isetan and Lido Cineplex which underwent a major refurbishment and now houses 11 cinemas including Singapore's first and only IMAX's Digital Theatre System.

Further on Scotts Road, past Royal Plaza on Scotts hotel, is the striking red **DFS Galleria ❿**, which stocks a wide variety of duty-free goods, from high-end clothing to kitschy souvenirs.

Far East Plaza

Take the overhead bridge to the **Far East Plaza ⓫**. Its eclectic hole-in-the-wall shops target teens looking for affordable streetwear but there is also no lack of bespoke tailors, tattoo parlours and karaoke pubs. Though the building has not worn its years well, it is still a great place for bargains.

Goodwood Park Hotel

Far East Plaza is sandwiched between **Goodwood Park Hotel ⓬** and the Grand Hyatt. Designed by Swan and MacLaren after the castles along the River Rhine, the Goodwood Park was originally built as the Teutonia Club in 1900 for the German community.

During World War I, the club was seized as an enemy property and then auctioned off to three Jewish brothers who turned it into a performance venue, christened Goodwood Hall. One of its highlights in 1922 was a performance by one of the world's greatest ballerinas, Anna Pavlova.

In 1929 the hall was converted into a hotel. The Japanese used it as their military headquarters during their occupation, and in 1945 the British turned it into a war-crimes court. Its Grand Tower, which became a national monument in 1989, has notable architectural elements such as fluted columns, delicate woodwork and graceful archways.

Grand Hyatt

On the other side of Far East Plaza is the **Grand Hyatt ⓭**, which has angled doors and a Zen-inspired fountain in its lobby. These features reportedly were designed to address *feng shui* concerns; the hotel's business is said to have boomed after they were installed.

THE MAIN STRETCH

At the junction of Scotts and Orchard roads is the pagoda-like **Marriott Hotel** ⓮. Adjoining it is **TANGS** department store, noted for its cult skincare brands and kitchen gadgets. Next door is **Lucky Plaza** ⓯. It is tatty around the edges but still popular for bargain electronic goods.

ION Orchard

Situated opposite TANGS is **ION Orchard** ⓰. This swanky mall houses flagship stores of numerous luxury brands such as Prada, Miu Miu, Marc Jacobs, and many food outlets. Head up to IONSKY at the 56th floor, the highest point on Orchard Road, for 360° views of Singapore through special telescopes.

Wisma Atria

Next to ION is the Orchard MRT station. Further on is the fashion-centred **Wisma Atria** ⓱, with a branch of the Japanese department store Isetan and numerous high-street fashion boutiques. A good lunch spot here is **Food Republic**, see ⓘ②.

Ngee Ann City

Linked by an underpass to Wisma Atria is the oversized **Ngee Ann City** ⓲, with boutiques selling everything from haute couture to street fashion. Its anchor tenant, **Takashimaya** department store, has a wonderful food hall, purveying delicacies from the world over, including England's Harrods and many fine Japanese brands. **Books Kinokuniya** on the third floor stocks all manner of books and magazines, and the fourth floor has art galleries and stylish stationers.

The Paragon

Unbridled consumerism continues across the road in **The Paragon** ⓳, filled with boutiques of top international designer names such as Gucci, Prada, Salvatore Ferragamo and Tod's. Located here as well are Marks & Spencer, Toys 'R' Us and a good range of eateries and patisseries.

Knightsbridge and The Heeren

Opposite The Paragon is Grand Park Orchard Hotels's Knightsbridge, housing retail stores such as Abercrombie & Fitch and Tommy Hilfiger. Further along is the teen magnet **The Heeren Shops** ⓴, selling trendy threads.

Mandarin Gallery

Opposite The Heeren is Meritus Mandarin Hotel and its stylish shopping arcade, **Mandarin Gallery** ㉑. There are various well-known boutiques here including one by local designer Ashley Isham. Food-wise,

Entrepreneur

TANGS was founded by C.K. Tang, who arrived in Singapore from China in 1922. He made his fortune peddling China-made lace from house to house. Among the first to recognise the potential of Orchard Road, the Christian was unperturbed by the presence of a Chinese cemetery opposite the store's location. In fact, business flourished and outgrew the original smaller building. TANGS is today one of Singapore's favourite home-grown retailers.

Food and Drink

② FOOD REPUBLIC

04-00 Wisma Atria; tel: 6737 9881; Mon–Thur and Sun 10am–10pm, Fri–Sat until 11pm; $

This massive food court's décor is reminiscent of the hawker set-ups of yesteryear. Retro-looking pushcarts offer dim sum and drinks, while a huge variety of stalls sell local food, alongside eight mini restaurants with a range of cuisines from Thai to North Indian.

Above from left:
signage at
Centrepoint; entrance
to a terrace house on
Emerald Hill;
Orchard Road is
Singapore's designer-
brand central.

Below:
Peranakan Place.

there are several good outlets such as the famous **Ippudo** ramen eatery from Japan, see ⑪③.

Tourist Information

Swing by the **Singapore Visitors Centre** ㉒ (daily 9.30am–10.30pm), at the junction of Cairnhill and Orchard roads, where you can get information on sights, book tours and purchase tickets to events.

EMERALD HILL

The Somerset MRT station is close by, if you want to call it a day. Opposite the station is **Peranakan Place** ㉓, a complex of highly ornamented Straits Chinese terrace houses. At its shaded terrace café, relax with a drink. Then go explore the lovely Chinese Baroque-style terrace houses further up the slope, on **Emerald Hill** ㉔.

Conservation Houses

The 30 double-storey terrace houses on Emerald Hill, built between 1901 and 1925, have thankfully not been razed but carefully restored, having been accorded conservation status in the 1980s, which means their owners are not allowed to alter their facades.

Today, although the interiors of most of these houses have been refurbished, their original facades remain well-preserved. Look out for ceramic tiles with intricate flower motifs, ornamental mouldings, and carved swing doors with gold patterns. Check out no. 83 for its original facade with pastel blue wood and white tiles, and no. 73, which has intricate gold paintwork on its wooden shutters.

The value of these houses is sky high, and many are rented out to well-heeled expatriates. You may be able to peek inside some of these plush homes

Food and Drink

③ IPPUDO
04-02/03/04 Mandarin Gallery, 333A Orchard Road; tel: 6235 2797; www.ippudo.com.sg; Mon–Sat 11am–11pm, Sun 11am–10pm; $$
This famous ramen eatery from Japan sees long queues at meal times, so get there early. Slurp up the famed authentic ramen in a creamy tonkotso broth brewed for over 20 hours.

④ QUE PASA
7 Emerald Hill Road; tel: 6235 6626; www.emeraldhillgroup.com; daily noon–2am; $$
Located in a Peranakan townhouse on Emerald Hill, this Spanish-inspired bar serves sangria and a good range of wines as well as delicious tapas.

if the doors are ajar. The majority of these upscale residences have a court-yard; a few of them even have small indoor swimming pools.

Watering Holes

There are also a few watering holes on Emerald Hill. Establishments such as **No. 5** (tel: 6732 0818), **Ice Cold Beer** *(see p.123)* and the atmospheric **Alley Bar** *(see p.123)* are longstanding favourites. **Que Pasa**, see ⑭④, is great for tapas and sangria.

CENTREPOINT

If you still have the time and energy for more shopping, step into the well-loved **Centrepoint** ㉕. Its main tenant is **Robinsons**, the oldest department store in Singapore, dating back to the 1850s. When its owners tried to sell it in 2003, infuriated shoppers petitioned against the sale – such is the loyalty it enjoys. It has the nicest sales staff around, and its biannual sales are eagerly anticipated.

Orchard Central

Opposite Centrepoint is **Orchard Central** ㉖, a retail development dedicated to Asian brands as well as **313 Somerset** ㉗ which also has a massive Food Republic Food Court. Somerset MRT is just below this mall.

DHOBY GHAUT

A 10-minute walk from Centrepoint, past the drab Orchard Plaza and Concorde Hotel takes you to the gate of the Istana ㉘, the Singapore president's official residence. Opposite is the leafy **Istana Park** ㉙, with pretty landscaping. Its centrepiece is the Festival Arch, a structure with banners, flags and a design that echoes the Istana entrance.

Beside the Istana is yet another mall, **Plaza Singapura** ㉚, with the French hypermarket Carrefour and other speciality shops. Next door is **The Atrium@Orchard** ㉛, linked to the Dhoby Ghaut MRT station by an underpass.

MacDonald House ㉝, one of the oldest multistorey office buildings in this area, next to The Atrium, and the adjoining buildings mark the end of Orchard Road.

Gluttons Central
The Orchard Central site, opposite Centrepoint, has an interesting history. In the 1970s it was Glutton's Square, a popular open-air street-dining spot. The food stalls were revived during the 2004 Singapore Food Festival but have since been relocated next to The Esplanade and renamed Makansutra Gluttons Bay *(see p.39)*.

The Istana

The Istana ('palace' in Malay) is the office and official residence of Singapore's president, S.R. Nathan, though he chooses to stay in his humbler abode in eastern Singapore. Built in 1869, the elegant neo-Palladian Anglo-Indian building was once the British governor's residence. During the Japanese occupation, it was used by Japanese army commanders. The grounds of the Istana are open to the public on New Year's Day, Hari Raya Puasa, National Day, Deepavali and Chinese New Year. Foreigners need to pay a $1 entrance fee. On the first Sunday of every month, a changing-of-guards ceremony takes place at the main gate from 6pm to 6.30pm. Check the dailies for details.

BOTANIC GARDENS AND TANGLIN VILLAGE

The Botanic Gardens, a lovely green lung minutes away from Orchard Road, has luxuriant trees, virgin jungle, and a fabulous orchid garden. Close by is Tanglin Village, with stylish restaurants and antiques shops.

DISTANCE 3.5km (2 miles)

TIME 3–4 hours

START Botanic Gardens

END Tanglin Village

POINTS TO NOTE

Do this walk in the early morning or late afternoon when the air is fresher and the weather cooler. The main Tanglin Gate entrance to the Botanic Gardens is at the junction of Holland and Napier roads. This walk starts the Central Core, accessed via the Nassim Gate entrance on Cluny Road. The nearest MRT station is Orchard. From there, take a taxi to the Visitor Centre at the junction of Nassim and Cluny roads.

Label Reading

In line with the education mission of the gardens, most trees are clearly labelled. Look out for the Cannonball tree *(Couroupita guianensis)*, with its hardy bright pink flowers and large heavy fruit hanging from its trunk, and the Monkey Pot tree *(Lecythis ollaria)*, whose fruit opens a lid to release its seeds when ripe.

Food and Drink 🍴

① CASA VERDE

Visitors Centre Singapore Botanic Gardens; tel: 6467 7326 www.lesamis.com.sg; daily 7.30am–11pm; $$

This al fresco spot is managed by the same people behind the fine-dining restaurant Au Jardin *(see p.120)*, It serves both local and Italian cuisine. Breakfast and an all-day dining menu including wood-fired pizzas are also available.

The first botanic garden in Singapore was established in 1822 on Fort Canning Hill by Stamford Raffles as an experimental station for evaluating crops for commercial cultivation. Its most notable crop was the Pará rubber tree *(Hevea brasiliensis)*, from Brazil, introduced by Henry Ridley, who went on to establish Malaya's rubber industry. This original garden was closed in 1829.

BOTANIC GARDENS

The present 64-hectare (158-acre) **Singapore Botanic Gardens** (tel: 6471 7361; www.sbg.org.sg; daily 5am–midnight; free) was founded by an agri-horticultural society in 1859 and subsequently handed over to the colonial administration for maintenance. Today the gardens contain over 3,000 species of trees and shrubs, in areas as varied as virgin jungle, marshland, lakes and formal gardens. It is also a centre for horticultural and botanical research and experimentation, with an emphasis in orchid breeding and hybridisation. The orchid programme can be traced back to the 1920s when Eric Holtum was the director of the gardens.

SINGAPORE BOTANIC GARDENS

Before you begin your walk, get a bite at **Casa Verde**, see ⑪①, located at the **Visitor Centre ①**. After your meal, go through the **Palm Court**, with cascading water features and palm trees, veer right and walk towards the Evolution Garden.

Evolution Garden

The **Evolution Garden ②** (daily 5am–7pm) is a cleverly designed garden, with landscaping that chronicles the evolution of plants from the pre-historic times till the present day. Rock formations are interspersed among ferns and trees that are rarely found on the streets of modern cities. Look out for the curious-looking giant clubmosses *(epidodendrons)*, the prehistoric equivalent of trees today, and stone columns of 'petrified' tree trunks, which are fossilised remains of ancient trees.

Leave the Evolution Garden and retrace your steps to the Palm Court and past a restored 1920s black-and-white colonial bungalow, which houses the fine-dining French restaurant Au Jardin *(see p.120)*.

Symphony Stage

Continue on Heliconia Walk. From here you can see the **Shaw Foundation Symphony Stage ③**, flanked by the **Symphony Lake** and the rolling lawns of the **Palm Valley**, which teem with picnickers during the occasional weekend concerts.

National Orchid Garden

Head down Upper Palm Valley Road to the **National Orchid Garden ④**,

(daily 8.30am–7pm; charge), whose landscaped grounds are filled with a profusion of gorgeous orchids. It has

Above from far left: orchid blooms; Botanic Gardens.

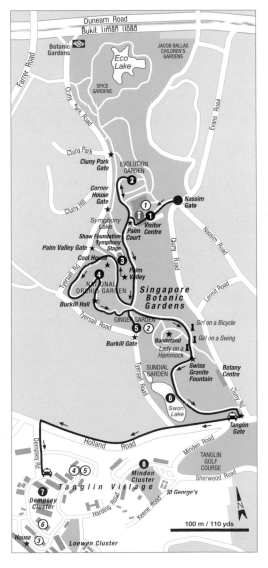

Above from left:
water features complement the lush greenery; strolling in the serene gardens.

National Flower
Look out for the *Vanda Miss Joaquim*. This hybrid was discovered by Agnes Joaquim in her garden in 1893 and was selected as Singapore's national flower in 1981 because of its hardiness and resilience.

Child's Play
The Jacob Ballas Children's Garden (Tue–Sun 8am–7pm; free), in the Botanic Garden's Bukit Timah Core, is a playground and nature park for kids. Interesting attractions include a treehouse, a photosynthesis corner and a sensory garden where kids can see, smell and touch plants. Adults can enter only if accompanied by a child below 13 years old or by a guide.

Right:
1930s bandstand.

the largest orchid display in the world with some 1,000 species and 2,000 hybrids, and more are added every year. The meandering paths and fountains make this a charming walk.

Highlights include the **VIP Orchid Garden**, with hybrids named after state dignitaries and VIPs, such as the *Dendrobium Margaret Thatcher* and the *Dendrobium Benazir Bhutto*. Next to the VIP Orchid Garden is **Burkill Hall**, a colonial plantation bungalow built in 1886. It is now used to showcase information on the different hybrids named after the VIPs who have visited the garden.

Don't miss the **Cool House**, a simulated tropical montane forest habitat, draped with orchids, epiphytes and carnivorous pitcher plants.

Ginger Garden

Continue to the **Ginger Garden** ❺ to see a collection of flora from the ginger

family, including bananas and heliconias. The restaurant **Halia**, see ⑪②, is located here.

Lower Ring Road

Take the Lower Ring Road, along which you will come across a white cast-iron **bandstand**, built in 1930.

Further down Lower Ring Road are a series of **bronze sculptures** by Sydney Harpley: *Girl on a Swing*, *Girl on a Bicycle* and *Lady on a Hammock*. Completed 1984–1989 and symbolising freedom and exuberance, they were gifted by David Marshall, Singapore's first chief minister, and are dedicated to the children of Singapore.

Swan Lake

Turn right when you come to the **Swiss Granite Fountain** and walk past the **Sundial Garden** to **Swan Lake** ❻, with a huge swan sculpture in its heart. Visitors, especially families with children, come here to feed the few swans and terrapins.

The path then brings you to the Tanglin Gate, from where you can exit the gardens.

TANGLIN VILLAGE

After your Botanic Gardens tour, hop on a taxi to **Tanglin Village** (www.tanglinvillage.com.sg), located off Holland Road (only about five minutes away), for lunch or dinner.

Originally a nutmeg plantation, the area was converted to the Tanglin Barracks, occupied by British troops, in the 1860s and was later abandoned. Of

late the barracks have been given a new lease of life and is now a thriving lifestyle and dining destination, organised into three clusters: Dempsey, Minden and Loewen.

Dempsey Cluster

The **Dempsey Cluster** ❼ (www.dempseyhill.com) is the most developed, with plenty of good restaurants and stores selling Asian-style furniture, artefacts and antiques amid lush greenery. A favourite among locals is the durian stall located at the car park. You can catch scents of the pungent fruit a distance away.

If you think you will need a rub down to soothe your muscles after your walk, book one at **House's Beauty Emporium** (8D Dempsey Road; tel: 6479 0070; www.dempseyhouse.com; daily 10am–9pm). Its Spa Esprit offers a comprehensive menu covering facials, massages, body treatments and foot spas. In the complex as well are two great places to unwind in: **Barracks Café** (tel: 6475 7787; Mon–Fri noon–6pm, Mon–Sun 6pm–10.30pm), which serves international cuisine in themed rooms, including a greenhouse, and **Camp Bar** (tel: 6475 7787; Wed–Thur 6pm–midnight, Fri–Sat 6pm-2am), which offers a range of classic cocktails.

Meal Stops

The Dempsey cluster offers a carefully curated selection of restaurants. Recommended are **Taman Serasi Food Garden**, see ⑪③, **Samy's Curry**, see ⑪④, **Long Beach Seafood**, see ⑪⑤, and **Margarita's**, see ⑪⑥.

Minden Cluster

The **Minden Cluster** ❽ is home to the Tanglin Golf Course and the Anglican **St George's Church** (tel: 6473 2877; www.stgeorges.org.sg), built in 1911 as a garrison church for British troops. During World War II, the Japanese army used it as an ammunition store. This pretty red-brick building, designed in classical Romanesque style, was made a national monument in 1978.

Rainforest

The Botanic Gardens holds one of the city's two virgin rainforests (the other being Bukit Timah Nature Reserve, see p.91), in its Central Core. Divert from the suggested walk through this 6-hectare (150-acre) patch to see rattan, ferns and canopy trees.

Food and Drink

② HALIA
Ginger Garden, Botanic Gardens; tel: 6476 6711; www.halia.com.sg; Mon–Fri noon–11pm, Sat–Sun 10am–11pm; $$–$$$
Halia ('ginger' in Malay) is nestled amid lush tropical foliage. Lunch is a lighter menu of Western fusion fare. For dinner there is a Continental menu of sublime ginger-inspired dishes.

③ TAMAN SERASI FOOD GARDEN
01-12, Blk 9 Dempsey Road; tel: 6476 1512; www.jonesthegrocer.com; Mon 9.30am–6pm, Tues–Fri 9.30am–11pm, Sat–Sun 9am – 11pm; $$
This Australian gourmet store with a café is a great place for a coffee and a sweet treat or a light lunch.

④ SAMY'S CURRY
01-03, 25 Dempsey Road; tel: 6472 2080; daily 11am–3pm and 6–10pm, $$
Delicious South Indian fare is served on banana leaves. Samy's has a faithful following for its fish-head curry.

⑤ LONG BEACH SEAFOOD
01-01, 25 Dempsey Road; tel: 6323 2222; www.longbeach seafood.com.sg; daily 11am–3pm and 5.30pm–1.30am; $$$
Excellent Singapore-style seafood dishes, including black pepper crab, chilli crab and fried baby squid.

⑥ MARGARITA'S
01-19, 11 Dempsey Road; tel: 6471 3228; Tue–Sun 11.30am–3pm and 6–10pm; $$$$
Cool down with a margarita while waiting for your Tex-Mex dishes. The enchiladas, with swimmer crabmeat, pinto beans and Spanish rice, are a must-order.

KAMPONG GLAM

The Arab Quarter has shed its sleepy image with the entry of stylish boutiques and cafés, but its Malay and Middle Eastern essence can still be felt in the dignified mosques and traditional businesses.

DISTANCE 1.5km (1 mile)

TIME 3–4 hours

START Arab Street

END Bali Lane

POINTS TO NOTE

This is recommended as a late-morning-to-afternoon walk as many of the shops only open for business in the afternoon. Take a taxi to Arab Street or the MRT to the Bugis station and walk for 15 minutes to the starting point.

By the Coast

This neighbourhood used to run along the shore, with many of its houses built on stilts above the tidal mudflats. Much of Kampong Glam was mangrove swamp and was drained in the 1820s. Beach Road, as its name suggests, was once a coastal road. In the 1880s reclamation pushed the road further inland.

Stamford Raffles allocated this area to Sultan Hussein, the Malay king who ceded the island to the British in 1824. The sultan built a palace here for his family and homes for his retainers. Subsequently Javanese and Minangkabau traders, Arab textile merchants and even Chinese tombstone makers settled here, alongside the Malay community.

The enclave's name means 'village of the *gelam* tree'. The tree's bark was prized for its medicinal value and used by the early Bugis and Malay residents to caulk boats, although it would be difficult to find this tree here now.

Today's Kampong Glam extends over the area bordered by Ophir Road, Victoria Street, Jalan Sultan and Beach Road. Its main landmarks are centuries-old mosques, but lately, it has also drawn a new following with local designer boutiques, cafés and restaurants.

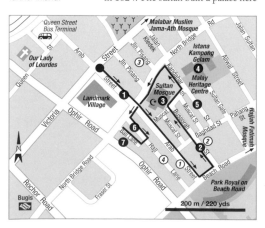

ARAB STREET

Start your stroll on **Arab Street ❶**. These shops and eateries here are set in restored two-storey shophouses, many of which were built in the Early Shophouse style in the 1840s, resembling unadorned dollhouses with their squat upper levels and simple lines.

Along Arab Street are shops selling ethnic jewellery, alcohol-free perfumes and all manner of fabrics. At the corner of Arab and Baghdad streets is **Rishi Handicrafts** (no. 58), its shopfront displaying baskets and other caneware of every shape, size and colour. Opposite Rishi is **Goodwill Trading** (no. 56), its walls covered with batiks. There are also several shops along this street selling Oriental carpets. For a quick bite, try **Café Le Caire**, see ⑪①.

BUSSORAH STREET

Turn left on Beach Road and pass the fishing tackle shops. Turn left again, onto the narrow **Bussorah Street ❷**, lined with souvenir shops. During the Ramadan fasting month before the Muslim celebration of Hari Raya Puasa each year, this street bustles with food vendors and their Muslim customers, who buy home-cooked delicacies for breaking their fast at sunset. At other times it is a peaceful lane. On the right is **Alaturka**, see ⑪②, serving delicious Turkish cuisine.

Further along at no. 21 is a Malay food stall that has been in business without a name on its signage for more than three decades. Many locals come for its *teh tarik* ('pulled' tea), *teh halia* (ginger tea), *nasi lemak* (rice cooked in coconut milk), *pisang goreng* (banana fritters) and Malay cakes.

Past the Bussorah Street junction is **Bussorah Mall**, a quiet pedestrianised street flanked by restored 19th-century shophouses. Sultan Mosque looms at the end of the street.

SULTAN MOSQUE

Sultan Mosque ❸ (tel: 6293 4405; www.sultanmosque.org.sg; Mon–Thur, Sat–Sun 9am–4.30pm, Fri 9am–noon and 2.30–4.30pm), distinguished by its golden onion dome and soaring minarets, is the most important place of Muslim worship in Singapore. The first mosque on this site was built in 1824 by Sultan Hussein. The current structure, the largest mosque in Singapore with a 5,000-capacity prayer hall, was completed in 1928. The colonial architect firm Swan and Maclaren

Above from far left: shophouses on Arab Street; Rishi Handicrafts' caneware.

Etiquette
You are welcome to step into the mosques but before entering, remove your footwear and ensure that your legs and arms are covered. Robes are usually available at the entrance. Photography is allowed but do be sensitive to the worshippers.

Food and Drink

① CAFÉ LE CAIRE
39 Arab Street; tel: 6292 0979; Mon–Fri noon–3.30am, Fri–Sat until 5.30am; $$
The dishes come in generous portions and are good for sharing. Try the mezze platter and *meshawi*, with aromatic grilled meat and vegetables. If you prefer to dine in air-conditioned comfort, head upstairs to the cosy dining room.

② ALATURKA
16 Bussorah Street; tel: 6294 0304; daily 11am–11pm; $$
This charming place serves authentic Turkish fare such as mezze with dips, fluffy pide (Turkish version of pizza), kebabs, and *sütlaç*, a milky Turkish rice pudding. After your meal, have a cup of apple tea or strong Turkish coffee.

adopted the design of the Taj Mahal in India and combined it with Persian, Moorish, Turkish and classical themes. One of Sultan Hussein's descendants, Tengku Alam, is buried in a private grave in the grounds.

MALAY HERITAGE CENTRE

Leave the mosque and turn left onto Kandahar Street. Here stands the **Istana Kampong Gelam**, set in a beautiful garden (daily 8am–9pm; free)

and currently being redeveloped. Its architecture combines traditional Malay motifs with the Palladian style that dates back to the 1840s. It was once the palace of Sultan Ali Iskandar Shah, son of Sultan Hussein.

Housed in the Istana building is the **Malay Heritage Centre** ❹ (tel: 6391 0450; www.malayheritage.org.sg; Mon 1–6pm, Tue–Sun 10am–6pm; charge) due to reopen in 2012 after major works. It has nine galleries showcasing interesting regalia of the Malay royalty and artefacts pertaining to Malay history and culture. The adjacent two-storey **Gedung Kuning** ('Yellow Mansion'), built for Tengku Mahmoud, grandson of Sultan Hussein, is now Tepak Sireh restaurant (*see p.121*).

KANDAHAR STREET

Walk down **Kandahar Street** ❺ towards North Bridge Road. The old shophouses here have been accorded conservation status. Their architecture is a fusion of European, Malay, Chinese and Indian elements. Look out for the units with swinging doors known as *pintu pagar*.

If you have not had lunch, cross North Bridge Road and turn left towards **Jalan Pisang**. At no. 11 on this street is the **Hajjah Maimunah Restaurant**, see ⑪③.

HAJI LANE

Continue on North Bridge Road, go past Arab Street and turn onto **Haji Lane** ❻. Here are some seriously hip

---

Historical Mosques

Apart from the grand Sultan Mosque, there are two other mosques in the Arab Quarter that are worth detours. At the corner of Jalan Sultan and Victoria Street are the golden domes of the blue mosaic-tiled Malabar Muslim Jama-Ath Mosque (tel: 6294 3862; daily 10am–noon and 2–4pm, *below*). The mosque, established by Indian Muslims from the Malabar coast of Kerala, harks back to the time Kampong Glam was founded. Historical records dating from 1836 show that Malay princes were buried in the old Malay cemetery here. Behind Jalan Sultan and off Beach Road is Hajjah Fatimah Mosque (tel: 6297 2772; daily 9am–9pm), named after a devout Muslim shipping entrepreneur who donated her home to be the site of this mosque. Designed by a British architect, this European-style building, completed in 1846, features a tall minaret and a stained-glass dome. Because its spire tilts at six degrees, the mosque is dubbed Singapore's 'Leaning Tower'.

boutiques opened by young local designers and vintage stores dripping with bohemian charm. Pop into **Know It Nothing** (no. 51; tel: 6392 5475; www.knowitnothing.com, daily 1–8pm) for men's apparel, shoes and accessories. Its owner-designer Suraj Melwani crafts shirts under his own label and sells cult fashion sourced from all over the world.

Dulcet Fig (no. 41; tel: 6396 5648; dulcetfig.com; Mon–Thur 1–9pm, Fri–Sat until 10pm, Sun 2–6pm) and **Pluck** (no. 31; tel: 6396 4048; pluck.com.sg; Mon–Sat 1–8pm) have vintage clothing, handbags and soft furnishings. Pluck's ice-cream parlour is a delightful nook to rest your legs.

At one end of Haji Lane is **Salad** (no. 25/27; tel: 6299 5805; Mon–Sat noon–8pm), with home and fashion accessories as well as clothes in mainly black and white colours. Its homeware is imported from Thailand, Vietnam and Cambodia, while apparel and bags originate from Hong Kong and Korea.

A few doors from Salad is **Altazzag Egyptian Restaurant**, see ⑪④, which serves delicious Middle Eastern fare.

BALI LANE

Take the small lane that leads from Haji Lane to **Bali Lane** ❼. A nice end to your afternoon is **Blu Jaz Café** (no. 11; tel: 6292 3800; www.blujaz.net; Mon–Thur noon–midnight, Fri until 2am, Sat 4pm–2am), a casual restaurant-bar. Linger around or return in the evening to catch its live jazz performances.

To leave this area, cross Ophir Road, parallel to Bali Lane; the Bugis MRT station is just ahead.

Food and Drink 🍽

③ HAJJAH MAIMUNAH RESTAURANT
11 Jalan Pisang; tel: 6291 3132; Mon–Sat 7.30am–9pm; $
This small, modest eatery has a fierce following so it is usually full. Join in the queue and make your choices at the counter. The spread includes tender beef *rendang* (dry curry) stewed in coconut milk, grilled chicken and colourful Malay cakes.

④ ALTAZZAG EGYPTIAN RESTAURANT
24 Haji Lane; tel: 6295 5024; Sun–Thurs 4pm–4am, Fri, Sat 4pm–5am; $$
This modest restaurant serves reasonably priced fare, such as the Egyptian mixed grill with various types of kebabs.

10 LITTLE INDIA

A walk through the most characterful ethnic enclave in Singapore, to discover spirited daily life, heady aromas of spices and enchanting traditional rituals. Experience the heart of Singapore's Indian culture with all your senses.

DISTANCE 1.5km (1 mile)
TIME 2–3 hours
START Little India Arcade
END Leong San See Temple
POINTS TO NOTE

Late morning is a good time to start this tour. Take a taxi or the MRT to the Little India station, a short walk to the starting point.

Above from left: colourful floral garlands; intricate images at Sri Veeramakaliamman Temple.

Deepavali
October or November is one of the best times to visit the area, as the whole place is dressed and lit for the Festival of Lights celebrations.

Little India spreads over the area bounded by Sungei Road, Jalan Besar, Lavender Street and Race Course Road. Through its heart runs **Serangoon Road**, a thoroughfare from which numerous backlanes, lined with small shops spilling over with saris, fabrics and floral garlands, fan out.

The enclave was designated by Stamford Raffles as the Indian district in his 1822 town plan, first thriving as a cattle-rearing ground. It later grew as a hub of Indian commerce, just as it still is today, although many of the traditional businesses have made way for contemporary ones. Little India is a magnet for both migrant workers and tourists from the Indian subcontinent.

BACKSTREETS

Begin your tour at the Art Deco-style **Little India Arcade ❶**. Spend some time perusing the stalls selling crafts, jewellery and souvenirs. Exiting the mall, turn left on **Clive Street**, where little shops are crammed with cookware.

Turn left onto **Campbell Lane ❷**. In the arts and craft shops here, you can find a jumble of rugs, soft furnishings, trinkets, Christian icons and Buddha and Ganesh images. At **Jothi Store & Flower Shop** (no. 1; tel: 6338 7008; www.jothi.com.sg; Mon–Sat 9am–9pm, Sun 8pm), fragrant jasmine flowers are strung into garlands, to be offered in Hindu temples.

Turn right onto Serangoon Road, which is dotted with restaurants, some of them established since the time when the area was largely populated by single men, whose domestic arrange-

Food and Drink

① ANANDA BHAVAN
58 Serangoon Road; tel: 6297 9522; daily 7.30am–10pm; www.anandabhavan.com; $
Established in 1924, Ananda Bhavan serves South Indian vegetarian dishes, like crispy *thosai*, a pancake made of rice and gram flour, eaten with lentil gravy or filled with spicy potato curry.

② KOMALA VILAS
76–78 Serangoon Road; tel: 6293 6980;
daily 11.30am–10:30pm; www.komalavilas.com.sg; $
This place is known for its cheap vegetarian Indian food and its many varieties of *thosai*. Fast-food style meals are served downstairs, and restaurant-style seating is available upstairs.

ments did not include private kitchens. Stop by **Ananda Bhavan**, see ⑪①, for ginger tea and South Indian snacks.

From Serangoon Road, turn right onto **Dunlop Street** ❸. You can see a typical provision shop with interesting Asian fruits and vegetables, from bitter gourd to betel leaves, heaped into crates and baskets that spill over onto the walkway. Spices such as bright yellow turmeric, deep red saffron and mellow brown cinnamon, assail your senses with their aromas and colours.

When you have seen enough of Dunlop Street, backtrack to Serangoon Road. This stretch of the thoroughfare contains shops selling multicoloured saris and accessories on both sides. Another Little India institution here is **Komala Vilas**, see ⑪②, with good vegetarian food.

SRI VEERAMAKALIAMMAN TEMPLE

Across the road, past Belilios Road, stands the **Sri Veeramakaliamman Temple** ❹ (tel: 6295 4538; www.sri veeramakaliamman.com; daily 5.30am–12.30pm and 4–9pm), dating from 1835. It is dedicated to the multi-armed goddess Kali, the manifestation of anger against evil; in one of her images she is shown ripping out the guts of a hapless victim. As consort to Shiva, Kali is also known as Parvati in her benign form. Therefore she is both feared as well as loved. In the main shrine, her statue is flanked by those of her sons – Murugan, the child god, and Ganesh, the Elephant God.

The temple is packed with devotees on the Hindu holy days of Tuesday and Friday. They often break a coconut before entering to denote the breaking of their ego. Cracked shells are tossed into the aluminium receptacles under the *gopuram* (tower). Fresh coconut and mango leaves above the entrance symbolise purity and welcome; the lotus represents human striving for spiritual perfection; and banana offerings indicate abundance.

Beauty Salons
Salons on Buffalo Road offer henna tattooing, oil massages and herbal hair treatments. Try Susiee House of Beauty (no. 32A; tel: 6292 6720) and Rupini's (no. 24–26; tel: 6291 6789).

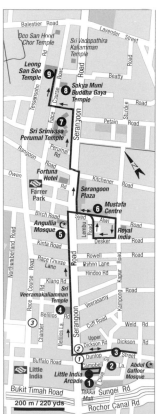

Abdul Gafoor Mosque
Tucked away at 41 Dunlop Street is this Arabian- and Renaissance-style mosque (tel: 6295 4209; daily 7am–noon and 2.30–4.30pm), built in 1859. Its prayer hall is decorated with Moorish arches and has a tableau tracing the origins of Islam.

Bars

Little India has its share of interesting nightspots. One of them is Prince of Wales (101 Dunlop Street; tel: 6299 0130) is a casual backpacker's pub with Australian draught beers, barbecues and live rock and folk music.

ANGULLIA MOSQUE

Continue on Serangoon Road to Birch Road, with another historical place of worship, the **Angullia Mosque** ❺ (tel: 6295 1478; daily 4.30–8am and noon–10pm), built over 100 years ago. Cross over to the other side to Syed Alwi Road and visit the decidedly secular phenomenon that is **Mustafa Centre** ❻ *(see feature box, below)*.

Turn right onto **Kampong Kapur Road**, where the garish Royal India Hotel stands, and right again onto **Desker Road**. This street has plenty of cheap hotels and a seedy reputation. Turn right onto **Lembu Road**, where Indian migrant workers in the con-

struction industry congregate on the **Lembu Road Open Space**.

SRI SRINIVASA PERUMAL TEMPLE

Turn left onto **Syed Alwi Road** and make your way to Serangoon Road. It is a good 10-minute walk to the next place of interest. After passing Fortuna Hotel and the Kitchener Road junction, cross to the opposite side. After Perumal Road is the brightly coloured **Sri Srinivasa Perumal Temple** ❼ (tel: 6298 5771; daily 6.30am–noon and 6–9pm). It was founded by migrant Naradimhaloo Naidu, who endowed a portion of his property to the temple in 1860. A century later, local philanthropist P. Govindasamy Pillay met the expenses for adding the five-tier *gopuram* (tower), which rises 21m (70ft) above the entrance. Figures on the *gopuram* depict the various incarnations of Vishnu, also known as Perumal, the Preserver of Life, who appears on Earth in different forms.

Thaipusam

Each year during Thaipusam, around January or February, a procession of devotees begins at the Sri Srinivasa Perumal Temple and ends at the Chettiar Temple on Tank Road. The men pierce their tongues, cheeks and bodies with skewers that support their *kavadi*, heavy arched steel structures decorated with peacock feathers. Women devotees participating in the procession carry jugs of milk on their heads. These acts of faith are performed

Mustafa Centre

Mustafa Centre (145 Syed Alwi Road; tel: 6295 5855; www.mustafa.com.sg; daily 24 hours) is a department store like no other in Singapore. Open around the clock, it stocks the widest selection of merchandise, from the latest power tools to the most obscure toiletries, heaped bazaar-style. The Mustafa success has spawned a hotel, café and travel agency, plus an extension of the mall on Verdun Road. The best time to shop here is the wee hours of the morning when the aisles are nearly empty, and the worst is Sunday, when it is really crowded.

either as penance or in gratitude to Lord Murugan, Shiva's son.

Leave the temple and follow the adjacent path, past blocks of public housing and a tiny playground, to **Race Course Road**.

SAKYA MUNI BUDDHA GAYA TEMPLE

Little India may be the hub of the Hindu community, but, reflective of Singapore's multicultural nature, it also has places of worship of various faiths.

To your right is the **Sakya Muni Buddha Gaya Temple** ❽ (tel: 6294 0714; daily 8am–4.45pm), which is also known as the Temple of 1,000 Lights because the 15m (50-ft) -high statue of the seated Buddha is surrounded by a halo with that many light bulbs. Inside the door is part of a branch from the sacred bodhi tree under which the Buddha is said to have attained enlightenment. Worshippers may illuminate the lights around the statue for a small donation. There is also an enlargement of the Buddha's footprint, inlaid with mother-of-pearl.

LEONG SAN SEE TEMPLE

Further down the road on your left are some lovely old houses and the **Leong San See Temple** ❾ (no. 371, tel. 6298 9371; daily 6am–6pm) with an ornately carved roof. The temple is dedicated to Guan Yin, the Goddess of Mercy. Its altar also has an image of Confucius; the temple is hence popular with parents who bring their children to pray for success in examinations.

Have a meal at one of the popular restaurants on Race Course Road, such as **Banana Leaf Apolo**, see ⑪③, before you call it a day. The Farrer Park MRT station is nearby.

Above from far left: blowing his trumpet at the Sri Srinivasa Perumal Temple; street scene; jewellery boxes.

Below: giant Buddha image at the Sakya Muni Buddha Gaya Temple.

Food and Drink 🍴

③ BANANA LEAF APOLO
54–58 Race Course Road; tel: 6293 8682; www.thebananaleafapolo. com; daily 10am–10pm; $$
The fish-head curry is a must-try, as is the mutton or chicken *biryani* (basmati rice cooked with spices), served on banana leaves. A range of North Indian dishes are available too.

SENTOSA

Sentosa, the largest of Singapore's offshore isles, is a recreational playground for everyone, with amusement rides and theme park-style attractions for families with children, and nice white-sand beaches for sun worshippers.

DISTANCE 4km (2½ miles)
TIME A full day, or overnight
START Resorts World Sentosa
END Songs of the Sea
POINTS TO NOTE

The fastest way to the island is to take the Sentosa Express light rail (daily 7am–midnight; charge) from VivoCity mall on the mainland. It takes less than 5 minutes to reach Imbiah Station. To get to VivoCity, take the MRT to HarbourFront station. You can also get to Sentosa by taxi, cable car (tel: 6270 8855; www.mountfaber.com.sg; daily 8.30am–10pm; charge) or by the SIA Hop-on Sentosa Shuttle (hotline: 9457 2896; www.siahopon.com; daily 9am–9pm; charge). Look out for the SIA Hop-on at stipulated bus-stops along Orchard Road, Marina Bay area, Boat Quay, Clarke Quay and Chinatown. On the island, you can walk, or take the light rail or the free bus services and beach trams. Otherwise, board the Sentosa Rider www.sentosarider.com; daily 9am–10.30pm; charge) from Orchard Road, Chinatown and Marina Bay. Alternatively, get to the island on foot via the Sentosa Boardwalk. Stroll from VivoCity's waterfront promenade to Sentosa along a covered travellator (daily 7am – midnight).

Entrance Fees

If you take the Sentosa Express to the island, the entrance fee is included in the fare of S$3. If you walk via the Boardwalk, the entrance fee is S$1. Those who take a taxi will be charged either S$2, $3, $5 or $6 per taxi depending on the time and day. Most of the individual attractions have separate admission fees, which can add up if you are bringing your family, so take advantage of 'package' tickets with entrance to multiple attractions at discounts. Call 1800-736 8672 for more information.

Sentosa (tel: 1800-736 8672; www.sentosa.com.sg), located to the south of the main island, was once known as Pulau Blakang Mati ('island at the back of death' in Malay) because of the frequent outbreaks of fatal disease. Before it was turned into a leisure playground and renamed Sentosa, which means 'isle of peace and tranquility' in Malay, it was at different times a refuge for pirates, a military garrison, and a detention centre for citizens arrested under the Internal Security Act.

Far from being a place that invokes contemplation, Sentosa is filled with activities and attractions. While some welcome its theme park atmosphere, others have criticised its lack of focus. It has something for everyone, from historical sights to laid-back beaches to child-centric attractions.

Over-nighter

It would be too exhausting to see all the attractions in a single day. This itinerary covers the highlights. If you are inspired to see more, stay overnight at one of the hotels or resorts *(see p.115)*.

Resorts World Sentosa

After an extensive redevelopment, Sentosa today is a must-visit spot especially for families. The sprawling 'integrated resort' **Resorts World Sen-**

tosa **❶** (www.rwsentosa.com) boasts a casino, mid-range and upscale hotels and restaurants as well as a slew of high-end boutiques. The biggest draw here is the Universal Studios theme park, the only one in Southeast Asia.

The nearest train stop is Waterfront Station. Hop off and have breakfast at **Toast Box**, see **🍴①**. Then head to **Universal Studios Singapore** (tel. 6577-8888, open Mon–Sun 10am–7pm; charge). You can spend an entire day exploring the seven zones and 24 themed rides, of which 18 are exclusively designed for Singapore. Highlights include Shrek's 4-Adventure,

Above from far left: performance at the Dolphin Lagoon; the Merlion and the Sentosa Express; Tiger Sky Tower; Hollywood Boulevard at Universal Studios Singapore.

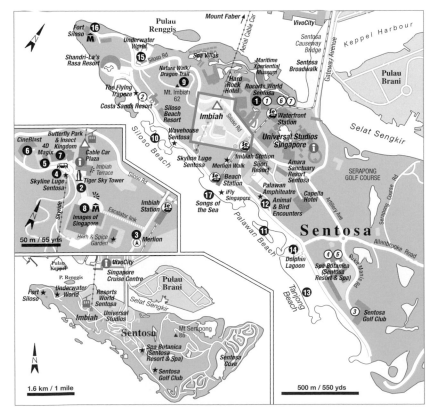

Flying Trapeze
If you want to fly like
a circus performer,
head to Siloso
Beach's Flying
Trapeze (Tue–Fri
4–6pm, Sat, Sun
and public holidays
4–7pm; charge).
An instructor will be
at hand to supervise
your 'stunt'.

Below: beach
volleyball action
on Siloso Beach.

Jurassic Park Rapids Adventure, Madagascar's tropical jungle based on the DreamWorks movie, Ancient Egypt with the *Revenge of the Mummy* ride, and the Battlestar Galactica, the world's tallest pair of duelling rollercoasters. Online pre-booking is usually necessary, especially during the busy school holidays.

Other attractions include a Marine Life Park, touted as the world's largest oceanarium. The resort will also boast the world's longest man-made rainforest river, the Maritime Xperiential Museum and the world's first 4D multi-sensory typhoon theatre. You can easily spend an entire day here.

IMBIAH LOOKOUT

Bird's-Eye Views
To enjoy great views of the Singapore harbour and the surrounding islands, there are two options close to Imbiah Station, though worth ascending only on clear days. One is the 110m (360-ft) **Tiger Sky Tower** ❷ (daily 9am–9pm; charge), whose lift whisks you up for a view from 131m (430-ft) above sea level. The other is the 37m (120-ft) **Merlion** ❸ (daily 10am–8pm; charge), which is also the focus of a show with smoke and laser lights at night.

Thrill Rides
Kids and thrill-seekers will like the **Skyline Luge Sentosa** ❹ (daily 10am–9.30pm; charge). After buying your ticket at the booth near Beach Station, ascend a slope by a four-seater chairlift and whizz down a 650-m/yd paved track in a luge, which is a cross between a go-kart and a toboggan.

Near the top of the Skyride is **Sentosa 4D Magix** ❺ (daily 10am–9pm, last show at 8.45pm; charge), with an engaging 4D movie experience. More gripping action is found at the high-tech **Sentosa CineBlast** ❻ (daily 10am–9pm; charge), located behind 4D Magix.

Butterfly Park & Insect Kingdom
For something more subdued, stroll through the lush grounds of the **Butterfly Park & Insect Kingdom** ❼ (daily 9.30am-7pm; charge), located next to 4D Magix. As many as 1,500 butterflies from more than 50 species, including some endangered ones, flutter around in this conservatory. It is also home to over 3,000 species of insects.

Images of Singapore

The best attraction in the Imbiah cluster is **Images of Singapore** ❽ (daily 9am–7pm; charge). Housed in a former military hospital, this museum has waxwork exhibits that recount Singapore's social history.

Nature Walk

Nature lovers can explore the 1.5km (1-mile)-long **Nature Walk** ❾, which starts from the Cable Car Arrival Plaza. Wander through a secondary rainforest and look out for vegetation such as the insectivorous pitcher plants and huge Tembusu trees.

BEACHES

Although the views are somewhat marred by container ships in the distance, Sentosa's beaches are probably Singapore's finest stretches of sand, running some 3km (2 miles) along the southern shore of the resort island and interspersed with scenic lagoons and coconut groves.

Siloso Beach

Siloso Beach ❿ is a hotspot for watersports and beach volleyball. From here you can head out to sea on rental windsurfers, canoes and pedal boats, join bare-chested young men and bikini-clad ladies for a game of volleyball, or chill out at **Trapizza**, see ⓕ②, a nice spot for a cool beer and lunch.

Adventure-seekers can free-fall through the air at **iFly Singapore** (tel: 6571 0000; www.iflysingapore.com; Mon–Fri 10am–11pm, Wed, Sat–Sun 9am–11pm; charge), the world's largest themed wind tunnel for indoor sky-diving. The flying height is equivalent of five storeys and you will also enjoy panoramic sea views. This attraction is located beside the Beach Station. About five minutes' walk from this station is **Wavehouse Sentosa** (tel: 6377 3113; www.wavehousesentosa.com; Mon 10.30am–10pm, Tues–Sun 9am–10pm; charge). There, surfers, both novices and experts, can enjoy riding 10-foot man-made waves. After hanging up your wetsuit, you can sip cocktails, have a bite, and listen to live music.

Palawan Beach

Over at **Palawan Beach** ⓫, a few attractions are suitable for families with kids. You can climb onto the **suspension bridge**, which links the main island to a tiny islet billed as the southernmost point of continental Asia. On the islet are two towers, clad in wood and bamboo, that afford a view of the sea. Near the beach is the Palawan Amphitheatre, the venue of **Animal & Bird Encounters** ⓬, where the audience can snuggle up to snakes, primates and birds during performances.

> ### Food and Drink 🍴
> ② TRAPIZZA
> Siloso Beach; tel: 6275 0100; www.shangri-la.com; daily 11am–9.30pm; $$$
> Trapizza is an outdoor Italian-style restaurant run by Rasa Sentosa Resort. Its menu includes pizzas, pastas and other casual fare. There is also a children's set menu.

Above from far left: resident of the Butterfly Park & Insect Kingdom; relaxing amid nature; Palawan Beach.

Beach Transport
A tram plies the three beaches daily from 9am to 7pm.

Tropical Spa
Those who seek some pampering may wish to make an appointment at the Spa Botanica (tel: 6371 1318; www.spa botanica.com) at The Sentosa Resort & Spa. Besides mud pools, float pools with cascading waterfalls and meditative labyrinths, the spa offers every conceivable treatment, from scrubs and massages to herbal wraps and aromatherapy facials.

Reflexology
Try fish reflexology at the Underwater World. This spa therapy was first discovered in the Middle East. Immerse your feet in a warm pool and tiny Turkish spa fish swim up and gently nibble at your feet, removing dead skin. A qualified foot reflexologist then gives you a relaxing foot massage.

Below: waxworks and guns at Fort Siloso.

Tanjong Beach

On the eastern side of Sentosa is **Tanjong Beach** ⓭, a more peaceful and secluded spot removed from the madding crowd, great for relaxing with a book and cool drink.

DOLPHIN LAGOON

Along Palawan Beach also sits the **Dolphin Lagoon** ⓮ (daily 10.30am–6pm; charge includes entry to the Underwater World), where rare and intelligent pink dolphins, also known as Indo-Pacific Humpbacked Dolphins, present their tail-flapping antics in 'Meet the Dolphin' shows (11am, 1.30, 3.30 and 5.30pm). If you book ahead (tel: 6275 0030; extra charge), you can have a closer encounter, including a swim in the lagoon with the dolphins. How does a 'dorsal tow' sound?

UNDERWATER WORLD

Your ticket to the Dolphin Lagoon also admits you into the **Underwater**

World ⓯ (www.underwaterworld.com.sg; daily 9am–9pm; charge), a sanctuary for more than 2,500 sea creatures, located on the western end of the island. As you journey through the 'ocean', or rather, an 83m/yd-long acrylic tunnel, on a travellator, you are surrounded by marine life of every imaginable kind, from stingrays and reef sharks to turtles and jellyfish.

Highlights

Highlights at the Underwater World include Gracie, a dugong, or sea cow, which was rescued as a calf off Pulau Ubin *(see p.90)*. The oceanarium also has the world's largest display of fearsome-looking Sand Tiger Sharks, their razor sharp teeth visible as they swim overhead.

Don't miss the Living Fossils exhibit, where about 20 fish, including the massive arapaima, which can grow up to 3m (10ft), and the pacu, a tamer cousin of the piranha, have been tagged with microchips. When a tagged fish swims past a sensor, information such as its species and origin is displayed on an LCD touchscreen.

FORT SILOSO

Near the Underwater World is another of Sentosa's history display and one of its must-sees, **Fort Siloso** ⓰ (daily 10am–6pm; charge). During World War II, the British pointed all their guns and cannons at this fort out to sea. This proved futile as the Japanese unexpectedly invaded overland from the north via the Malayan peninsula.

The armoury and cannons are still on display. The Surrender Chambers here bring to life Singapore's formal surrender to the Japanese in 1942 through a mix of gripping real audio-visual footage, artefacts and realistic wax figurines.

EVENING SUGGESTIONS

End the day at the **Songs of the Sea ⑰** (Siloso Beach; daily 7.40pm and 8.40pm, additional 9.40pm show on Sat; charge). With a live cast, dazzling lasers, pyrotechnics, water jets and fire set to rousing music, this show will enthral the little ones.

Dinner Options

Sentosa has no lack of dinner options, with a number of restaurants that are ranked among the best in Singapore. Recommended are **Il Lido**, see ⑪③, **The Garden**, see ⑪④, **The Cliff**, see ⑪⑤, **L'Atelier de Joël Robuchon**, see ⑪⑥, and **Singapore Seafood Republic**, see ⑪⑦.

Nightlife

Sentosa's nightspots are concentrated on the beaches. **Café del Mar** (tel: 6235 1296; www.cafedelmar.com.sg; Sun–Thurs 11am–11pm, Fri–Sat 11am–2am), on Siloso Beach, is a stylish franchise of the famous Ibiza original. Relax on a daybed or in a cabana facing the sea, or soak in a jacuzzi or the sunken pool with a swim-up bar. Order bar snacks and sangria to go with the sunset view. Palawan Beach's nightlife options

include **Bora Bora Beach Bar** (tel: 6278 0838; www.boraborasentosa.com), which has a great atmosphere and a wonderful drinks list.

Over at Tanjong Beach, party-goers can sip cocktails and enjoy the sunset at **Tanjong Beach Club** (tel: 6270 1355; www.tanjongbeachclub.com).

Above from far left: fun on the beach; *Songs of the Sea* multimedia show.

Food and Drink

③ IL LIDO
Sentosa Golf Club, 27 Bukit Manis Road; tel: 6866 1977; www.il-lido.com; daily 11.30am–2.30pm, 6.30pm–11pm. $$$$
Have drinks at the ultra-stylish lounge bar before you adjourn to alfresco seats for classic regional Italian fare and a fantastic view of the Singapore Straits at sunset.

④ THE GARDEN
Spa Botanica, The Sentosa Resort & Spa, 2 Bukit Manis Road; tel: 6371 1130; www.thesentosa.com; daily 10am–10pm; $$$$
Located in a bright and airy conservation building with alfresco seating by a pool. The 'conscious dining' menu focuses on wholesome, fresh produce and light, natural flavours.

⑤ THE CLIFF
The Sentosa Resort & Spa, 2 Bukit Manis Road; tel: 6371 1425; www.thesentosa.com; daily 6.30pm–midnight; $$$$
Amid The Cliff's romantic setting by the sea, dine on the finest seafood as well as contemporary creations prepared in the show kitchen. There is also an extensive selection of French oysters.

⑥ L'ATELIER DE JOËL ROBUCHON
26 Sentosa Gateway, Resorts World, Hotel Michael; tel: 6577 7888; daily 5.30pm–10.30pm, $$$$
Sit around the counter and watch chefs rustle up the finest dishes and tastings menus at the energetic open kitchen. It's all about interactivity here between the waitstaff, chefs and guests.

⑦ SINGAPORE SEAFOOD REPUBLIC
26 Sentosa Gateway, Resorts World #01-292 Waterfront; tel: 6265 6777; singaporeseafoodrepublic.com; daily noon–3pm, Mon–Fri 6pm–11.30pm, Sat–Sun 5.30pm–11.30pm; $$$
A collaboration between various top restaurant names such as Tung Lok, Palm Beach, Seafood International and Jumbo, this seafood joint offers the best signature dishes such as chilli crab and other classic Singaporean seafood cuisine.

SOUTHERN ISLANDS

Around Sentosa is a cluster of islets known as the Southern Islands, comprising Kusu, a place of rest and worship; St John's, a holiday spot with an easygoing air; and Sisters' Islands and Pulau Hantu, both popular diving areas.

> **DISTANCE** 13km (8 miles) round trip
> **TIME** Half a day
> **START/END** Marina South Pier
> **POINTS TO NOTE**
> To get to the Marina South Pier, take bus no. 402 from the Marina Bay MRT station.

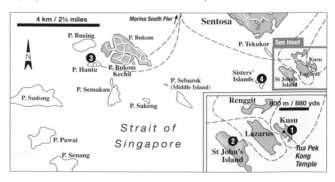

Tortoise Sanctuary
Pilgrims to Kusu Island release terrapins for good luck.

Pack a Picnic
There are no food and drink vendors on the islands, except Kusu during the pilgrimage season. It might be a good idea to pack a picnic when visiting these islands. More importantly, keep yourself hydrated and avoid overexposure to the sun.

You could do this tour on your own. A ferry service, which first stops at St John's Island followed by Kusu Island, is run by **Singapore Island Cruises** (tel: 6534 9339; www.island cruise.com.sg). To get to Sisters' Islands or Pulau Hantu, you will need to charter a boat.

A more leisurely way to enjoy views of Singapore's harbour and the soaring cityscape from the sea is the 2½-hour Imperial Cheng Ho cruise on a replica Chinese junk, operated by **Watertours Pte Ltd** (tel: 6533 9811; www.water tours.com.sg). Choose from packages that include breakfast, high tea or light refreshments, as well as a pick-up service from selected hotels or the Marina Bay MRT station. The cruise departs from the Marina South Pier and makes a half-hour stop at Kusu Island, passing St John's and other scenic islands along the way.

KUSU ISLAND

Kusu ❶, which means 'Tortoise Island' in the Chinese Hokkien dialect, is located about 6km (3½ miles) south of the Singapore island. Legend has it that two shipwrecked sailors, a Malay and Chinese, were saved by a tortoise that transformed

itself into an island. Each man gave thanks and built a place of worship according to his own belief.

Chinese Temple

The Taoist **Tua Pek Kong Temple** was actually built by a well-to-do merchant in 1923. It has classical Chinese green-tiled roofs and red walls and is reached via a series of pavilion-studded bridges set over a picturesque lagoon. Besides the Tua Pek Kong, the God of Prosperity, Guan Yin, the Goddess of Mercy, is also enshrined here. Also check out the **Tortoise Sanctuary**, filled with hundreds of tortoises. There is also a wishing well.

Muslim Shrines

Climb 152 steps to the summit of the hill. Standing here are three Muslim *keramat* (shrines), built to pay tribute to a devout man, Syed Abdul Rahman, his mother and sister, who lived in the 19th century. These are popular with childless couples who come to pray for fertility.

Best Time to Visit

About 130,000 worshippers throng Kusu during the ninth lunar month of the calendar, usually between September and November. So if you don't fancy crowds, avoid this period. During other times of the year, the island is idyllic with only about a dozen or so visitors on weekdays and some families on weekends. The island can be effortlessly covered on foot in less than an hour.

Day-trippers can enjoy a dip in the two lagoons, which are also good spots

for picnicking. There are many shady trees and picnic tables as well as public toilets and showers. As the food centre is only utilised during the annual pilgrimage, it is best to pack your own food and drinks for a picnic.

Overnight stay is not allowed on Kusu Island, so don't miss the last ferry back to Singapore island.

ST JOHN'S ISLAND

Situated approximately 6.5km (4 miles) south of Singapore, the 39-hectare (96-acre) **St John's Island** ❷ is a peaceful getaway with sandy beaches, lagoons, holiday bungalows and plenty of flora and fauna. This was where Raffles' ship anchored before he met the Malay chief on Singapore island in 1819. St John's served as a quarantine centre for immigrants until the 1950s before it was used as a holding centre for political detainees.

PULAU HANTU AND SISTERS' ISLANDS

Pulau Hantu ❸ (Ghost Island), to the northwest of Sentosa, was named so because it was said to be haunted by the spirits of two ancient warriors who fought to their deaths here. Enveloped by coral reefs, it is regarded as one of Singapore's best diving spots.

Singapore's richest coral reefs line the coasts of the two isles collectively known as **Sisters' Islands** ❹, which lie to the west of St John's Island. The currents can get pretty strong here so be cautious when swimming.

Above from far left: the Imperial Chong Ho cruise; roof details of a pavilion at the Tua Pek Kong temple on Kusu Island

Stay Overnight Those who want to experience an overnight stay on St John's Island can book the Holiday Bungalow, which comes with a kitchen and houses 10 persons, or the Holiday Camp, which can accommodate up to 60 persons. Bookings and immediate payment must be made personally at the Sentosa Express station at VivoCity (tel: 1800-736 8672; daily 9am–8pm).

Camping For overnight camping (bring your own equipment) on Sisters' Islands and Pulau Hantu, you must obtain prior approval from Sentosa (email: administrator @sentosa.com.sg).

WESTERN SINGAPORE

This part of the island has several attractions worth seeing, especially if you have kids in tow. The Jurong BirdPark and the Science Centre appeal to inquisitive minds, while the Chinese Garden offers quiet respite.

DISTANCE Varies, depending on the number of sights visited
TIME A full day
START Jurong BirdPark
END Singapore Science Centre
POINTS TO NOTE

These three attractions are not located near each other. So if time is limited, choose those that interest you most. To get to the bird park, take the MRT to the Boon Lay station and transfer to bus no. 194 or 251. A daily bus service (tel: 6753 0506; charge; check the bird park's website for details) also picks up visitors from VivoCity and bus stops near selected downtown hotels. To continue to the Science Centre from the Chinese Garden, take a taxi or the MRT to the Jurong East station and transfer to bus no. 335.

Park Hopper
Buy the 3-in-1 Park Hopper ticket package if you intend to visit the Singapore Zoo and the Night Safari *(see p.93)* as well. The ticket allows admission to the three parks at a lower combined price.

Above from left:
residents of the Jurong BirdPark; Chinese-style architecture and twin pagodas at the Chinese Garden.

Western Singapore, although designated as the country's industrial zone, has sprawling green spaces and a few family-friendly theme parks.

JURONG BIRDPARK

The 20-hectare (49-acre) **Jurong Bird-Park ❶** (2 Jurong Hill; tel: 6265 0022; www.birdpark.com.sg; daily 8am–6pm; charge) is home to some 4,600 birds across 380 different species. The landscaped grounds make for a pleasant walk. You can also hop onto the air-conditioned, elevated **Panorail** (separate charge) for more dramatic views.

Bird Shows

Check the information board for the show times and plan your route accordingly. The highly entertaining shows include the **Fuji World of Hawks**, starring magnificent condors, falcons, owls and other birds of prey. Another show sure to be a hit with the little ones is the **Birds 'n Buddies Show** (daily 11am and 3pm), with 13 costumed bird characters performing with live birds.

Highlights

As you walk in from the entrance, you will see the **Penguin Coast** which houses six species of penguins including the regal King Penguin and the tiny

Fairy Penguin. Other attractions include the Parrot Paradise with the park's most colourful and friendly residents and the **Pelican Cove**, where visitors can view underwater feeding of pelicans.

The **Southeast Asian Birds Aviary** is a lush walk-through rainforest with a simulated thunderstorm at noon. Look out for the feeding areas, where fruit is placed; there will be a flurry of activity around these spots in the trees.

Another outstanding attraction is the **Lory Loft**, a walk-in aviary hosting some 1,000 free-flying lories. From the boardwalk and the suspension bridge 12m (40ft) above ground, you take in 360-degree views of the simulated Australian Outback while you try to spot these birds with the most vivid plumage.

Around the walk-in **Waterfall Aviary**, with the thunderous man-made **Jurong Falls**, birds originating from Africa and South America fly free. You can also experience the billowing mist and the bird calls from inside the Panorail, which glides into the aviary.

Kiosks around the park offer snacks and light meals. Otherwise, have a bite at **Bongo Burgers**, see 🍴①.

CHINESE GARDEN

A short taxi ride from the bird park is the **Jurong Lake**, the setting for the **Chinese Garden ②** (1 Chinese Garden Road; tel: 6261 3632; daily 6am–11pm; free). Its theme gardens, fashioned in the style of the Summer Palace in Beijing, are a harmonious blend of natural and man-made elements such as rocks, ponds, streams,

bridges and footpaths. The lovely twin pagodas have nice views of the lake.

Don't miss the **Bonsai Garden** (daily 9am–5pm; free), a Suzhou-style garden with a pair of prized 200-year-old *Podocarpus* trees shaped like lions.

SCIENCE CENTRE

Move on to the **Science Centre ③** (15 Science Centre Road; tel: 6425 2500; www.science.edu.sg; daily 10am–6pm; charge), which has a mind-boggling 1,000 science exhibits in its 14 galleries.

Highlights include the **Genome Exhibit**, where DNA structures are explored through 3D exhibits. Optical illusions are found in the **Mind's Eye Gallery**, and children will find the sculptures and water features in the **Kinetic Garden** especially engaging.

The adjacent **Omni-Theatre** screens IMAX movies (Mon–Fri 10am–6pm, Sat–Sun 10am–8pm; charge).

If you are hungry after your visit, take a taxi to the IMM Building, 5 minutes from the Jurong East MRT station, to **Crystal Jade Dining Place**, see 🍴②.

Good to Go
In September and October every year, the Chinese Garden is ablaze with pretty lanterns for the annual Mid-Autumn Festival celebrations.

Zen Garden
The Japanese Garden (tel: 6261 3632; daily 6am–7pm; free) is connected to the Chinese Garden by a bridge. It has calming features like Zen rock gardens, stone lanterns, ponds and shrubs.

Food and Drink 🍴

① BONGO BURGERS
Jurong BirdPark; tel: 6265 0022; Mon–Fri 9.30am–6.15pm, Sat–Sun 8.30am–6.30pm; $$
Burgers in generous American-sized servings, plus a selection of other dishes like jumbo hot dogs and fish and chips.

② CRYSTAL JADE DINING PLACE
01-101 IMM Building, 2 Jurong East Street 21; tel: 6567 8010; www.crystaljade.com; Mon–Fri 11am–10pm, Sat–Sun 10.30am–10pm; $$
This casual family restaurant offers delicious dim sum, noodle dishes and other Cantonese-style snacks.

SOUTHERN SINGAPORE

The summit of Mount Faber is an ideal spot to take in panoramic views of Singapore's harbour. After the sun has set, swing by VivoCity, the city's largest mall, for a shopping spree or a meal at one of its many eateries.

Southern Ridges
The Marang Trail is part of a 9km (5½-mile) walk across Mount Faber, Telok Blangah Hill and Kent Ridge, collectively known as the Southern Ridges. Along the walk are two unique bridges, the Alexandra Arch and the Henderson Waves.

DISTANCE 1.5km (1 mile)

TIME Half a day

START Mount Faber

END VivoCity

POINTS TO NOTE

Start this tour in the late afternoon. To get to the top of Mount Faber, take a taxi or the cable car from Harbour-Front. At weekends, bus no.409 (www.sbstransit.com.sg/parks; Sat–Sun noon–9pm) departs from the Harbour-Front Bus Interchange every 30 minutes. You can also ascend on foot on one of its eight paths. Recommended here is the Marang Trail.

Although most well known for the Port of Singapore and as the gateway to Sentosa *(see p.72)*, southern Singapore is also an entertainment destination with a number of nightlife venues. Hike up Mount Faber, whose peak has a few dining outlets with a view, and then descend to the city's largest shopping mall, VivoCity, at the foot of the hill.

MOUNT FABER

Mount Faber ❶ is a 110m (360-ft) -high hill blanketed by one of the oldest rainforests in Singapore. Formerly called Telok Blangah Hill, it was renamed in 1845 after Captain C.E. Faber of the Madras Engineers, who built the road up to the summit.

Exit the HarbourFront MRT station from Exit D to Marang Road. This road leads to the **Marang Trail**, with stairs and shaded footpaths weaving through a secondary forest. The walk takes 15 to 20 minutes. The Marang Trail connects to Faber Walk, leading to the cable car station and **The Jewel Box** (tel: 6270 8855; www.mountfaber.com.sg; daily 8.30am–11pm) on the summit.

The Jewel Box is named for its jewel-box-like architecture. From here, enjoy vistas of the harbour and the city, especially delightful at sunset. Enjoy a pre-dinner cocktail and tapas at Moon-

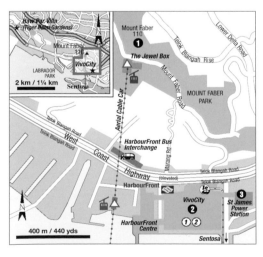

stone. There is also live music on Fridays and Saturdays (daily 6pm till late).

When you have had your fill of the views, retrace your steps down the hill or, if it is the weekend, take bus no. 409 back to the HarbourFront Bus Interchange. Across the road from the bus terminus is VivoCity. For something a little more dramatic, opt for a cable-car ride down to HarbourFront.

VIVOCITY

Inspired by the waterside location, Japanese architect Toyo Ito created a fluid facade that evokes sea waves for **VivoCity** ❷ (1 Harbourfront Walk; tel: 6377 6860; www.vivocity.com.sg; daily 10am–10pm). It has hundreds of stores and restaurants; in fact this mall is so huge you will need more than half a day to cover it thoroughly. It is best to return at another time, but for now, browse at leisure or head to one of its many food and beverage outlets such as **The Queen and Mangosteen**, see ⑪①, or **Signatures by Tung Lok**, see ⑪②.

Nightlife
After dinner, join in on some clubbing action at **St James Power Station** ❸, an enormous, nine-venue nightclub housed in a former coal-fired power station *(see p.123)*. An overhead bridge links the mall to the club.

Above from far left: Sapphire restaurant in The Jewel Box; VivoCity.

Not for the Acrophobic Take in views of the twinkling skyline while you dine in a cable car drifting between Mount Faber and Sentosa 70m (230ft) above the sea. Reservations (tel: 6377 9688; www.mountfaber.com.sg) are required for this Sky Dining experience.

Food and Drink 🍴

① THE QUEEN AND MANGOSTEEN
#01-106-107 VivoCity 1, Harbourfront Walk; tel: 6376 9380; Sun–Thur 11am–11pm, Fri–Sat 1am, Sun 11pm; $$
This British gourmet pub overlooks the waterfront and Sentosa Island. The kitchen dishes out pub grub in the form of miniature beef burgers, bangers and mash, and other creative bites. Pair your meal with Pimm's and Lemonade or craft brews.

② SIGNATURES BY TUNG LOK
01-57 VivoCity; tel: 6376 9555; www.tunglok.com; Mon–Sat 11.30am–3pm and 6–10.30pm, Sun 11am–2.30pm and 6–10.30pm; $$$
Signature dishes from the well-loved Tung Lok group's traditional Chinese restaurants are served in a chic decor surrounded by nice harbour views.

Haw Par Villa

Also known as Tiger Balm Gardens, Haw Par Villa (meaning 'villa of the tiger and the leopard') was named after its owners, Aw Boon Haw ('gentle tiger') and Aw Boon Par ('gentle leopard'), the brothers behind the famous Tiger Balm ointment. Built in 1937, the park features grotesque statues that illustrate Chinese mythological stories and notorious crimes. When Boon Par died in 1945, Boon Haw turned it into a public park. With its stagnant ponds and faded statues, the park has definitely seen better days, but it is a quirky sight whose gaudiness has to be seen to be believed. To get to the park (262 Pasir Panjang Road; tel: 6872 2780; daily 9am–7pm; free), take bus no. 188 from the HarbourFront Bus Interchange or bus no. 200 from the Buona Vista MRT station.

KATONG AND THE EAST COAST

Known for laid-back, beachside living, Katong in eastern Singapore is also a veritable living museum of Straits Chinese culture, with decades-old Peranakan eateries and floridly decorated conservation terrace houses.

Above:
architectural details in Joo Chiat.

DISTANCE 2km (1¼ mile), more if you want to explore the East Coast Park

TIME A half/full day

START Kuan Im Tng Temple

END East Coast Park

POINTS TO NOTE

Take a short taxi ride from the Paya Lebar MRT station to Tembeling Road.

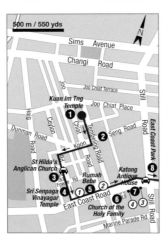

Katong is roughly bounded by Tanjong Katong Road, Mountbatten and East Coast roads, Changi Road and Telok Kurau Road.

In the early 19th century, Katong was situated just by the sea. Portuguese and Chinese settlers planted cotton, coconut and gambier in the area, whose name was derived from a species of sea turtle that was once found in Singapore. After World War I, it became home to well-heeled Chinese, Eurasians and Peranakans.

Due to land shortage in the 1970s, this area was reclaimed, all the way to the East Coast Parkway. Today Katong still counts among its residents well-to-do and distinguished folks, such as Singapore's president *(see p.59)*.

JOO CHIAT

The first stop of the walk is **Kuan Im Tng Temple ❶** at no. 62 on Tembeling Road, which is parallel to Joo Chiat Road. This ornate temple, with dancing dragons adorning its roofs and pillars, was built in 1921. It is dedicated to Buddhism, Taoism and Confucianism, with the Jade Emperor, the Goddess of Mercy (Guan Yin), the God of War (Guan Di), and several other deities enshrined in the prayer hall. Note its courtyard wall of Chinese paintings, illustrating classic stories of filial piety.

KOON SENG ROAD

Exit the temple and turn right on Tembeling Road. When you come to **Koon Seng Road ❷**, turn right. The row of prewar conservation terrace houses is a perfect showcase of the flamboyant Peranakan architectural style. Before World War II, many wealthy Peranakans built lavish homes that displayed a unique fusion of Chinese, Malay and European design elements. Typically these houses are underscored by plasterwork with flora and fauna motifs and intricate tiles, and feature a pair of carved wooden *pintu pagar* ('fence doors').

Continue to Joo Chiat Road, where you can hire a taxi to get to the next stop, Ceylon Road. If you choose to go on foot, note that it will be a lengthy walk with not much, except bungalows and apartment blocks, to see.

ST HILDA'S CHURCH

At the junction of Ceylon and Fowlie roads stands the 1934 **St Hilda's Anglican Church ❸** (42 Ceylon Road; tel: 6344 3463; daily 9am–6pm). Fashioned after an English parish church, the building is topped by a Victorian-style conical tower and features beautiful stained glass.

SENPAGA TEMPLE

A 5-minute walk from St Hilda's Anglican Church is one of Singapore's oldest Hindu shrines, the **Sri Senpaga Vinayagar Temple ❹** (19 Ceylon Road; www.senpaga.org.sg; daily 5.30am–12.30pm and 5.30–11pm). It dates back to the 1850s, when a statue of Lord Vinayagar, the Elephant God, was unearthed by the side of a pond. A Ceylonese (Sri Lankan) Tamil built the first temple structure, which was a simple shelter with a thatched *attap* (nipa) roof, positioned under a *senpaga* (Chempaka) tree. When the area was bombed during World War II, the main shrine remained intact. Today the temple, rebuilt in 1989, is an important place of worship for the Hindu community living in the east. It is noted for its 20m (65ft) high *gopuram* (tower), above its entrance, which bears 159 sculptures of Hindu gods and deities.

EAST COAST ROAD

After your temple visit, continue on Ceylon Road to **East Coast Road**. Stop by **Kim Choo Kueh Chang**, see ⑪①, for authentic Peranakan fare. An institution in Katong, Kim Choo was started by Madam Lee Kim Choo in the late 1940s. She first learned her

> ### Food and Drink 🍴
> #### ① KIM CHOO KUEH CHANG
> 109–111 East Coast Road;
> tel: 6440 5590; www.kimchoo.com;
> daily 8am–9pm; $$
> The must-try here are glutinous rice dumplings. The restaurant also serves homey Peranakan food; order the *assam* (tamarind) fish head with pineapple and vegetables, and vegetables stir-fried with sambal.

Above from far left: ornate terrace houses on Koon Seng Road; sculptures at the Sri Senpaga Vinayagar Temple.

Eurasians
The Katong area is also home to many Eurasians (descendents of intermarriages between Europeans and Asians). They were among Singapore's earliest immigrants, hailing from Malacca, Macau, Goa and Ceylon (Sri Lanka). With most of them as Roman Catholics, Christmas is a major celebration for this community. The Eurasian Heritage Centre (139 Ceylon Road; tel: 6447 1578; www.eurasians.org; daily 9.30am–6.30pm; free) offers insight into Eurasian culture.

Above:
embroidered Peranakan *kabaya* and vintage accessories at Kim Choo's gallery.

grandmother's secret recipe of making Peranakan glutinous rice dumplings at the age of 12, and supported her four children by selling these dumplings. She has since handed over her thriving business to them.

Peranakan Culture
Browse Kim Choo's retail corner with homemade cookies and condiments like *belacan* (prawn paste) and *taucheo*

(soy bean paste), which are indispensable for Peranakan cooking.

Upstairs is a gallery; Kim Choo's grandson, Raymond Wong, will gladly show you his collection of Peranakan artefacts, such as quality porcelain from Jiangxi, China, vintage batiks and intricate beaded slippers. One of the best souvenirs you can take away from here is a *sarong kebaya* (Nonya blouse and sarong skirt) with delicate embroidery. Demonstrations of dumpling-making are also offered here.

Just next door is **Rumah Bebe** ❺ (no. 113; tel: 6247 8781; www.rumah bebe.com; Tue–Sun 9.30am–6.30pm), a treasure trove of all things Peranakan, from furnishings and traditional apparel to jewellery and porcelain, housed in a 1928 shophouse. It is owned by former school teacher and renowned beadwork specialist Bebe Seet. Look out for the lovely bridal chamber on level two and intricate *kasut manik manik*, dainty slippers of fine beadwork. Bebe also conducts bi-weekly beading classes to keep the craft, which is on the brink of vanishing, alive.

Another stop for Peranakan treats is **Glory Catering**, see ⑪②.

Church of the Holy Family
East Coast Road is a long road. You can end your Katong tour after your meal, or further explore a couple of places more along the stretch.

Generations of Peranakan and Eurasian Roman Catholics living in the east have worshipped at the **Church of the Holy Family** ❻ (6 Chapel Road; tel: 6344 0046; www.

Food and Drink

② GLORY CATERING
139 East Coast Road; tel: 6344 1749; www.glorycatering.com.sg; Tue–Sun 8.30am–8.30pm; $–$$
Another old-time favourite, well loved for its *nasi padang* (rice with Indonesian-style dishes) and Peranakan sweet treats like pineapple tarts and other coconut-milk-infused cookies and cakes.

③ 328 KATONG LAKSA
216 East Coast Road; daily 9am–9pm; mobile tel: 9732 8163; $
Many eateries in this area claim that they serve the best laksa (thick rice noodles in a rich, spicy coconut-milk-based gravy). 328 Katong Laksa is largely acknowledged as one of the best.

④ CHIN MEE CHIN
204 East Coast Road; tel: 6345 0419; Tue–Sun 8.30am–5pm; $
This bakery and coffee shop hasn't changed much since it opened more than six decades ago. Loyal customers, spanning generations, have been coming here for coffee served in traditional porcelain cups, alongside soft-boiled eggs and *kaya* (coconut jam) toast. Traditional jam rolls, buns and cakes are popular for afternoon tea.

holyfamily.org.sg; daily 6am–7.30pm). In 1923 a chapel was built on this site and subsequently torn down to make way for this church, which was completed in 1932.

Antique House

Further down from the church is the **Katong Antique House** ❼ (208 East Coast Road, tel: 6345 8544; open by appointment only), an iconic shop owned by Peter Wee. He is a fourth-generation Baba who began his business of buying, restoring and selling Peranakan furniture, porcelain and other cultural products in 1971. The shop is a treasure trove of traditional crockery, jewellery, beaded slippers, costumes and furniture. A small gallery sits on the upper level of the shop-house. Peter has in-depth knowledge of his heritage, so make an appointment if you want to hear fascinating stories of yore.

A few doors down from the antique shop is **328 Katong Laksa**, see ⑪③, where you can enjoy the area's signature noodle dish. For something lighter, drop by **Chin Mee Chin**, see ⑪④.

EAST COAST PARK

Take a 5-minute taxi ride from East Coast Road to the **East Coast Park** ❽ further south. The beach park, stretching about 20km (12 miles) between the Changi Airport and Marina Bay, is a popular playground and dining destination.

The 7.5km (4½-mile) reclaimed beach is unfortunately just narrow slopes of not-so-fine sand, and the waters are rather murky and not recommended for swimming. Locals, however, don't complain, as the balmy environment, with views of ships anchored in the Strait of Singapore, is refreshing after a week of toiling in air-conditioned offices. At the weekends the park teems with picnicking families, joggers, campers, rollerbladers and cyclists. If you want to catch a glimpse of Singaporeans at play, the park is a good place.

Like elsewhere in Singapore, the East Coast Park offers plenty to eat. The restaurants at the **East Coast Seafood Centre**, famed for Singapore-style seafood dishes like chilli and pepper crabs, are persistently booked out *(see p.121)*.

Above from far left: beaded Peranakan slippers; Church of the Holy Family; Peranakan delights; rollerblading at the East Coast Park.

Watersports
Watersports facilities are available at the East Coast Park. The Mana Mana Beach Club (1212 East Coast Parkway, Area E; tel: 6339 8878; www.manamana.com) offers lessons and has boats, kayaks, SUP (stand-up paddle) boards and windsurfing boards for rental.

Left: Katong Antique House.

16 CHANGI

Peaceful Changi provides a welcome contrast to the frenzied city. Its star attraction is the poignant Changi Chapel and Museum, while laid-back Changi Village appeals with its restful and breezy atmosphere.

DISTANCE 5.5km (3½ miles)
TIME Half a day
START Changi Chapel and Museum
END Changi Beach Park
POINTS TO NOTE

Take a taxi to the Changi Museum or hop on bus no. 2 from the Tanah Merah MRT station. The bus stops opposite the museum. Take bus no. 2 from the same bus stop to Changi Village. To get to Pulau Ubin, walk to Changi Point Ferry Terminal (tel: 6542 7944), a few minutes from Changi Village Hawker Centre, and take a 10-minute bumboat ride (daily 6am – 8pm; 24 hours; charge; boats leave when there are 12 passengers).

Changi is most well known as the location of Singapore's airport, but it also contains a few gems worthy of a visitor's time and journey out of the city centre.

CHANGI CHAPEL AND MUSEUM

During the Japanese Occupation from 1942 to 1945, the Japanese army turned British-built barracks in Changi into a prisoner-of-war (POW) camp. It was a notorious hellhole where thousands of military and civilian prisoners were interned. They had to endure appalling conditions, described in a number of books, including *King Rat* by James Clavell, who was a POW at Changi.

Built in 1988, the **Changi Chapel and Museum** ❶ (1000 Upper Changi Road North; tel: 6214 2451; www.changimuseum.com; daily 9.30am–5pm; free) is dedicated to the POWs who were interned at Changi camp.

Museum Highlights

The **museum** provides moving insights into the POWs' lives in the Changi internment camp, which housed as many as 3,000 prisoners at one time. Among the exhibits are poignant letters, photographs, and personal effects donated by former POWs and their families, which portray the POWs' suffering and hope during those dark years. Especially notable are the sketches and paintings by William Haxworth and photographs by George Aspinall.

Changi Murals

The museum also features a replica of the Changi Murals. The Japanese military allowed a ward in the internment camp to be used as a chapel. Bombardier Stanley Warren, of the 15th Field Regiment, decorated the chapel with life-sized murals that depicted scenes

Original Murals
The original murals are now located within an operational military camp – Block 151 of Changi Airbase – and are open for public viewing only during four window periods in February, August, September and November. Visitors who wish to view them must apply at least two weeks ahead to the public relations department of the Ministry of Defence (email: prb@starnet.gov.sg).

from the life of Christ. These original murals, known as the **Changi Murals,** are now in the grounds of an operational military camp *(see margin, p.88)*. For many years after the war, the murals lay hidden and forgotten as the ward was used as a storage room, and were discovered during renovations in 1958. Warren returned to Singapore in 1963 and again in 1982 to restore the original murals.

Changi Chapel

The **Changi Chapel** is a replica of one of many similar places of worship erected by POWs while incarcerated in Changi camp. The original was dismantled after World War II and reassembled in Australia. This replica was built in 1988 in response to requests by former POWs and their families.

The chapel sits in a garden with hibiscus and frangipani plants. You are welcome to leave a flower on the altar or a note on a board to the left of the altar in remembrance of the POWs.

CHANGI VILLAGE

When you are done at the museum and chapel, hop on a 10–15 minute bus or taxi ride to **Changi Village ❷**. Along the way you can see Changi Prison and various military sites behind barbed wire fencing.

When you reach Changi Village, head to the **hawker centre**, see ⓘⓘ, located next to the bus terminus, for lunch.

Above from far left: notes left in remembrance of POWs at the Changi Museum; boats from the Changi Point jetty depart for Ubin island; the Changi Chapel.

Food and Drink 🍴

① CHANGI VILLAGE HAWKER CENTRE

2 Changi Village Road; daily early morning till late; $–$$
Recommended are Wing Kee (01-04) for its *hor fun* (flat rice noodles) with beef or seafood, and International (01-57) for its *nasi lemak* (coconut-flavoured rice) served with fried fish, peanuts, anchovies, egg and a spicy sambal sauce. But it is the two-decade-old Charlie's Corner (01-08; tel: 6542 0867) that is the outstanding favourite. Offering a huge selection of imported beer and old-school pub grub such as burgers, fried chicken wings and potato wedges, it gets really busy at the weekend. The stall is closed on Monday; that's when Charlie is out fishing.

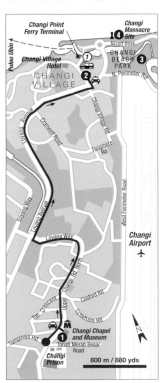

Above from left:
sailing, off Changi;
signage at the
beach park; treeshew
and visitor centre at
the Bukit Timah
Nature Reserve.

Take time to wander around the sleepy village, a slice of charming old Singapore. Shops such as George Photo (01-2000, Block 1) and the Salvation Army Thrift Shop (01-2078, Block 4), are tinged with nostalgia. Seafood restaurants and pubs also line Netheravon Road, while the **Changi Village Hotel** (tel: 6379 7111; www.changivillage.com.sg) offers the only hotel accommodation in the area.

Changi Village is also home to a variety of splendid old trees. The magnificent *Shorea Gibbosa* tree, which has a cauliflower-like crown, at the junction of Netheravon and Turnhouse roads, is said to be one of the last two left in Singapore.

A short walk from the hawker centre is the **Changi Point Ferry Terminal**, where you depart on a bumboat ride to **Pulau Ubin** *(see feature box, left)*.

Pulau Ubin

Located off Singapore's northeastern tip, Pulau Ubin (Granite Island) measures just 8km (5 miles) across and 1.5km (1 mile) wide. It is home to Singapore's last *kampung* (village), with about 100 villagers who still depend on well water and on diesel generators for electricity. Stop by the National Parks Board (NParks) information kiosk (tel: 6542 4108; daily 8.30am–5pm) to pick up a map and leaflets with details on the island's flora and fauna. In Ubin town are bicycle rental shops, eateries and provision shops. It is best to see the island on a bike; three cycling trails go past fruit and rubber plantations, mangrove swamps and quarry pits. On the eastern side of the island is Chek Jawa (daily 8.30am–6pm; *below*), a vast expanse of intertidal mudflats that teem with marine life, including endangered species. Visit during low tides; the area will be inundated at higher tides. NParks also conducts guided tours (charge) of Chek Jawa; the schedule is posted on its website (www.nparks.gov.sg).

CHANGI BEACH PARK

Take the footbridge to the 3km (2-mile) -long **Changi Beach Park ❸**. Changi Beach is a craggy stretch, so don't expect soft white sand under your feet. Higher tides can conceal sharp rocks; be careful and proceed slowly if you are wading in the water.

Still, the beach is popular with locals who come to picnic, fish at the pier, enjoy the sea breeze and watch planes land and take off from the Changi Airport.

The stretch of sea here is often dotted with dinghies and keelboats from the nearby sailing clubs.

Changi Massacre Site
Further east on Changi Beach is the **Changi Massacre Site ❹**, marked by a storyboard. This was where the sand was reported to have turned red with blood on 20 February 1942. Sixty-six Chinese men thought to be anti-Japanese sympathisers were lined up along the water's edge and killed by a Japanese firing squad.

BUKIT TIMAH NATURE RESERVE

Sanctuary to one of Singapore's two virgin rainforests and a rich biodiversity, this reserve is within easy reach of the city centre. Hike up to the hilltop for good views and spot tropical flora and fauna along the way.

Located almost in the geographic centre of Singapore, 12km (7½ miles) from the city, is the **Bukit Timah Nature Reserve** (177 Hindhede Drive; tel: 6468 5736; www.nparks.gov.sg; daily 6am–7pm; free). It has Singapore's highest hill, the **Bukit Timah Hill**, at 164m (538ft) above sea level and offers 164 hectares (405 acres) of ecologically important lowland rainforest. The hill is composed mainly of granite, and was once an active quarrying site in the mid-1900s.

BACKGROUND

Most of Singapore's forest was heavily logged until the mid-19th century. In 1884, in response to research commissioned by the Straits Settlements government on climatic changes arising from deforestation, the Bukit Timah Nature Reserve was established. For more than a century, the forest was a botanical collecting ground. The first known specimens of many species of Malayan plants were taken from here. The reserve has suffered significant changes both in its demarcated boundaries and biodiversity levels due to the poaching of animals and logging in the early 20th century and more recent

DISTANCE 1km (½ mile)

TIME 2–3 hours

START/END Bukit Timah Nature Reserve Visitor Centre

POINTS TO NOTE

This is best as a morning excursion. Allow 30 minutes to get there from the city centre. From the Newton MRT station, bus no. 67, 170 or 171 takes you to Upper Bukit Timah Road. Alight at Bukit Timah Shopping Centre, cross Jalan Anak Bukit, walk up Hindhede Road and then to the end of Hindhede Drive. Going by taxi is by far the easiest way. Have the driver drop you off at the car park.

Do Not Feed

Don't be tempted to feed the monkeys you encounter. The forest provides for them sufficiently and these monkeys have been known to behave viciously.

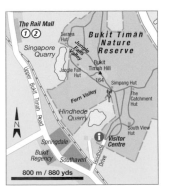

Before You Go

Wear comfortable clothing, sturdy shoes and scent-free insect repellent.

Above from left:
Bukit Timah quarry;
forest trail; baby
orangutan;
feeding time.

urban encroachments. Large mammals like tigers and deer no longer roam the forest, ecologically rare birds like hornbills and trogons, once part of the virgin rainforest, have vanished.

Rich Biodiversity

Still, nature lovers will not go away disappointed. There are over 2,000 native plants and 170 species of ferns recorded. Soaring dipterocarp trees are a feature of this reserve; there are more than 25 species. Don't expect to find the plants that feature in Singapore's urban greenery, though, as most of those are imported species. This is the real thing – you are looking at Singapore as she was in her earliest days.

The wildlife impresses with its variety. There are some 2 million insects and invertebrates, 660 types of spiders and 126 species of birds. Small

animals like squirrels, anteaters, treeshrews, long-tailed macaques have survived too, although it is not frequent that you get to see these animals.

Take time to pause and listen to the variety of bird song, usually in full chorus in the morning. Look out for any fruiting trees – figs in particular – around which birds flit and feast.

TRAILS

The **Visitor Centre** (daily 8.30am–6pm) at the foot of the hill is a good place to start. Orientate yourself and check out the hiking routes clearly marked on the map at the entrance.

You can find maps and directional signs along the trails. You can get to the summit and back in under an hour, if you take the shortest route at a brisk pace, or you can spend up to 3 hours covering more of the reserve. In wet weather, some of the paths can be muddy and involve scrambling over fallen tree trunks, but it is all part of the fun if you are prepared for it.

The first part, straight up a paved road, can be disappointing, but once past this, you are in a primary rainforest complete with a heavy canopy at the uppermost layer, rattans and liana vines at mid-level, and red ginger flowers and dark purple bat lilies on the forest floor. On the summit, enjoy views of the surrounding rainforest and **Seletar Reservoir** to the north.

On leaving Hindhede Drive, take a short taxi ride to the Rail Mall for lunch at **Sweet Salty Spicy**, see 🍴①, or **Galbiati**, see 🍴②.

Rare Find
Look out for the
Dillenia grandifolia,
a rare find in the
Bukit Timah Nature
Reserve, mainly
because this tree
with stilt roots is
usually found on
swampy ground.
The stilt roots of this
particular tree are
so tall that a person
can stand
under them.

Food and Drink 🍴

① SWEET SALTY SPICY
The Rail Mall, 392 Upper Bukit Timah Road; tel: 6877 2544; Mon–Fri 11am–2pm, Sat–Sun 11am–4pm and 6–10pm; $$
Thai-style meals in this contemporary deli-café. Try the Wagyu beef salad and the green curry with snapper and apple eggplants.

② GALBIATI
The Rail Mall, 400 Upper Bukit Timah Road; tel: 6462 0926; www.galbiatigourmet.com; Mon–Fri 11am–10pm, Sat–Sun 10am–10pm; $$
Italian chef-owner Roberto Galbiati helms this deli with freshly baked breads to go with hearty soups. Antipasti, pizzas and pastas are available too.

MANDAI

Lush Mandai is the setting of the Singapore Zoo, where animals roam in naturalistic enclosures, and the one-of-a-kind Night Safari, with nocturnal wildlife prowling in the moonlight.

An outing to see animals in cages is probably not most people's idea of fun. But the Singapore Zoo and the Night Safari, known to be among the most thoughtful zoo settings in the world, provide quite a different experience altogether. The 'open concept' of both zoos allows animals to roam freely in naturalistic habitats. Visitors are separated from most of the animals by only water moats and other low barriers.

SINGAPORE ZOO

The 90-hectare (220-acre) **Singapore Zoo ❶** (tel: 6269 3411; www.zoo.com.sg; daily 8.30am–6pm; charge) is nestled in a rainforest and displays some 2,500 animals representing 315 species, 29 percent of which are threatened. There is a lot to see at the zoo, so this tour features just the highlights.

Before you begin, note the animal show and feeding times posted at the entrance, so you can plan your tour. Recommended animal shows are **Elephants at Work and Play**, which features these mammals moving logs, and **Splash Safari**, with antics by sea lions and jackass penguins. The most spectacular feedings are at the polar bear and lion enclosures. There is also a tram service (separate charge) that plies the zoo.

DISTANCE Varies, depending on how much walking you do in the zoos
TIME Half a day
START Singapore Zoo
END Night Safari
POINTS TO NOTE

Take either bus no. 138 from the Ang Mo Kio MRT station or bus no. 927 from the Choa Chu Kang MRT station. The two attractions are located next to each other on Mandai Lake Road. If you plan to visit both the Singapore Zoo and the Night Safari, get the 2-in-1 Park Hopper at a discounted package price. Aim to arrive at the Singapore Zoo around 3pm and then head over to the Night Safari at 6pm.

Orangutans

The zoo has the world's largest colony of Bornean and Sumatran orangutans, the result of a successful captive breeding programme. See these primates up close at two free-ranging areas, where they hang out, literally and figuratively, among tall trees and swing across vines.

You can also have a **Jungle Breakfast with Wildlife** (daily 9–10.30am) in close proximity to orangutans as well

Park Hopper

Buy the 3-in-1 Park Hopper ticket if you plan to visit the Jurong BirdPark *(see p.80)* as well. The ticket is valid for one month from the date of purchase.

Kids' World

At the zoo's Rainforest Kidzworld, children can hop on animal rides, run loose at a water playground and watch animal shows.

Research Centre

If you are not squeamish, the zoo's Wildlife Healthcare and Research Centre might be of interest. It has a public viewing gallery for visitors to observe animal surgery and treatment.

Ah Meng
The most famous and adored resident of the zoo was Ah Meng. The orangutan passed away at the age of 48 (95 in human years) in February 2008. She was the only non-human to receive the Special Tourism Ambassador title from the tourism board in 1992. Personalities she had met include Michael Jackson, Elizabeth Taylor and Britain's Prince Philip.

as other creatures like snakes and otters at Ah Meng Restaurant (Terrace). Book one day in advance (tel: 6360 8560).

Highlights

Explore rainforest ecosystems in the **Fragile Forest**, a re-created tropical jungle that is sanctuary to fauna as diverse as tamarins, lemurs, sloths, parakeets and butterflies.

The walkway leading to the **Tiger Trek** is so lush, you might even think you are in a tropical jungle. The exhibit is the habitat of the extremely rare Bengal white tigers.

Other themed areas worthy of your time include the **Great Rift Valley of Ethiopia**, where Hamadryas baboons dwell, the **Elephants of Asia**, reminiscent of the hills of Burma, and the **Australian Outback**, where kangaroos and wallabies prance around.

By 2012, the spotlight will be on the two giant pandas from China. On loan for a decade, the animals will be living in the zoo's new attraction, **River Safari**.

Dinner and Entertainment

After you are done with the zoo, move on to the Night Safari next door. For dinner, choose either **Ulu Ulu Safari Restaurant**, see ⑪①, or **Bongo Burgers**, see ⑪②. Another interesting dining option is the **Gourmet Safari Express** (tel: 6360 8560; daily 7–10pm; charge), where you can dine and take in the animal exhibits at the same time in the comfort of a tram. Book at least one week ahead.

NIGHT SAFARI

If you have been disappointed with disinterested animals in day zoos, it could be because 90 percent of tropical mammals are active only at night. At the 40-hectare (99-acre) **Night Safari** ❷ (tel: 6269 3411; www.nightsafari.com.sg; daily 7.30pm–midnight; charge), the first night zoo in the world, animals are seen at their most active, feeding, socialising and prowling. The 41 naturalistic habitats are unobtrusively lit with a

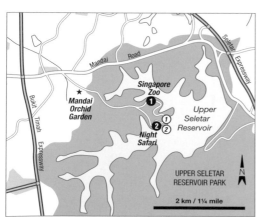

Food and Drink 🍴

① ULU ULU SAFARI
Night Safari; tel: 6269 3411; daily 6–11pm; $$
Try local cuisine like satay, fish tikka and *mee goreng* (fried noodles) in an ethnic-inspired setting.

② BONGO BURGERS
Night Safari; tel: 6269 3411; daily 6pm–midnight; $$
Dine on gourmet burgers, made with juicy meat patties that are chemical- and preservative-free. A Bornean tribal group entertains with blowpipe and fire-eating demonstrations.

gentle moonlight glow so the animals are not disturbed. Some 1,000 animals representing 120 species, of which 29 percent are endangered, roam the Night Safari. The night zoo has also been successful in breeding endangered species such as the anteater, giant flying squirrel, Malayan flying fox and spotted hyena.

Themed Exhibits

You can walk or travel around the eight themed exhibits, which are replicates of habitats found in Asia, Africa and South America, by tram (extra charge). The tram takes 45 minutes to complete the loop. As it moves along, your guide will point out the animals that come into view in a hushed tone. Flash photography harms the animals' eyesight in the long run and is hence not allowed.

Noteworthy exhibits include the **Himalayan Foothills**, with highland goats and sheep; the **Indian Subcontinent**, where striped hyenas coexist with lions; and the **Nepalese River Valley**, home to the greater one-horned rhinoceros and the golden jackal.

Don't miss the **Asian Riverine Forest**, where you can find **Chawang**, the Night Safari's icon, standing at close to 3m (10ft) tall and weighing about 3,500kg (3.5 tonnes). The largest and heaviest among all the animals at both zoos, this beautiful elephant is a rare 'crossed tusker', with tusks more than 1m (3ft) long.

Walking Trails

You can hop off at designated points along the tram route to divert on foot along three shorter trails: the **Fishing Cat, Leopard** and **Forest Giants trails**, where you can catch sight of smaller nocturnal creatures like the giant flying squirrel and mouse deer. The trails are clearly marked and rangers are stationed along the way to guide you.

Animal Show

After exploring the trails, end your night with the rousing **Creatures of the Night** show (daily 7.30pm, 8.30pm and 9.30pm; Fri–Sat and eve of holidays additional show at 10.30pm). This spectacular presentation showcases wolves and hyenas, as well as small animals like owls, raccoons and otters, all trained to entertain with clever tricks.

Above from far left: polar bear at the zoo; dining at the Night Safari; anteaters.

Best Time to Go
The Night Safari is extremely crowded at the weekend, so if you prefer a quieter visit, go on a weekday.

Orchid Garden

Some 200 varieties of orchids are cultivated in the Mandai Orchid Garden (200 Mandai Lake Road; tel: 6269 1036; www.mandai.com.sg; Mon 8am–6pm, Tue–Sun 8am–7pm; charge), located near the Singapore Zoo and the Night Safari. Wander around its Vintage Garden, spread over sloping terrain, to see a myriad of colourful orchids. Orchids are sturdy; if this is one of your last stops in Singapore, you can even bring home some, packed in boxes for your flight. The garden also grows a variety of herbs and has a tropical fruit orchard.

DIRECTORY

A user-friendly alphabetical listing of practical information, plus hand-picked hotels, nightspots and restaurants, clearly organised by area, to suit all budgets and tastes.

A–Z   98

ACCOMMODATION   110

RESTAURANTS   116

NIGHTLIFE   122

A

ADDRESSES

For high-rise apartments or buildings, addresses begin with the block or building number, then the street name and unit number followed by the postal code, e.g. Block 56, Bedok North Street 3, #03-04, Singapore 469623. For landed properties, the address is written as 52 Napier Road, Singapore 258500.

B

BUDGETING

Accommodation can cost anywhere from S$25 for a dorm room in a hostel and about S$120 for a room in a budget hotel to more than S$400 in a top-end luxury hotel. Food is cheap if you eat at hawker centres, usually about S$5, and so is public transport, less than S$2 per trip on the bus or train. Short taxi rides around the city centre will cost between S$8 to S$10. If you live frugally, it is possible to survive on a budget of less than S$100 a day. If you intend to live it up, be prepared to budget about S$50–60 for a 2–3 course meal (without drinks) and about S$30 for entry into clubs (inclusive of one drink). Set aside another S$30–40 per day for admission charges to attractions.

BUSINESS HOURS

Business hours are 9am–5pm Monday to Friday. Banks are usually open 8.30am–4pm on weekdays, and 8.30–1pm on Saturdays. Shops open from about 10am to 8pm daily (including Sunday) and many department stores are open until 9pm. Most Singapore Post branches in town are open from 8.30am to 5pm or 6pm on weekdays and from 8.30am to 1pm on Saturdays. Some Singapore Post outlets are open on Sundays too.

C

CHILDREN

Singapore is a safe place with plenty of family-friendly places. Some places in Singapore have attained the 'Pro-family Business' accreditation, such as the Singapore Zoo, Night Safari and several family-friendly malls. There are plenty of children's attractions, such as the Jacob Ballas Children's Garden at Botanic Gardens, Sentosa Island and those listed in the Western Singapore tour *(see pp.80–1)*. Children are usually given concessions for entrance fees.

CLIMATE

As Singapore is located 137km (85 miles) north of the equator, the weather usually varies between hot and very hot. Temperatures range between 33°C (91°F) and 24°C (75°F), with high humidity levels from 64 to 98 percent. Most of the rain falls during the northeast monsoon between November and February and to a lesser degree during the southwest monsoon from May to September. Thunderstorms, though, can occur throughout the year.

Minimum Age

To buy and consume alcohol and cigarettes, a person has to be 18 years old. The minimum age allowed in dance clubs is usually 18 for ladies and 23 for men. Some clubs allow anyone above 18 to enter.

CLOTHING

Smart-casual attire will see you through most occasions in Singapore, where normal office attire is shirt and tie for men, with jackets reserved for more formal occasions. Dress to cope with the heat when outdoors and have a wrap or light cardigan for the sharp drop in temperature inside some air-conditioned buildings. Shorts and T-shirts are acceptable in many places, although many clubs and some restaurants have stricter dress codes.

CUSTOMS

Visitors carrying more than the equivalent of S$30,000 in cash or cheque have to declare this fact to the customs authorities upon arrival. Duty-free allowance per adult is 1 litre of spirits, 1 litre of wine or port and 1 litre of beer, stout or ale. No duty-free cigarettes are allowed into Singapore although they may be purchased on the way out. Duty-free purchases can be made both upon arrival and departure except when returning to Singapore within 48 hours. This is to prevent Singaporeans from making a day trip out of the country to stock up on duty-free goods. Passengers arriving from Malaysia are not allowed duty-free concessions.

The list of prohibited items includes drugs (the penalty for even small amounts can be death), firecrackers, obscene or seditious materials, endangered wildlife or their by-products, reproduction of copyright publications, video tapes, video compact discs, laser discs, records or cassettes, chewing tobacco and imitation tobacco products, cigarette lighters of pistol or revolver shape, and chewing gum (except dental or nicotine gum). For more information, contact **Immigration & Checkpoints Authority** (www.ica.gov.sg) and **Singapore Customs** (www.customs.gov.sg).

D

DISABLED TRAVELLERS

There is a growing awareness of the special needs of disabled people. The **National Council for Social Services** (tel: 6210 2500; www.ncss. org.sg) is a good information source. The **Disabled People's Association of Singapore** (tel: 6899 1220; www.dpa. org.sg) has a booklet titled *Access Singapore*, which gives details of facilities for the disabled. Some of the newer buildings are designed with the disabled in mind but generally, getting around by public transport for the wheelchair-bound is a problem. There are some taxis that are large enough to accommodate wheelchairs but these have to be booked ahead.

E

EMBASSIES

Australia: 25 Napier Road, tel: 6836 4100
Britain: 100 Tanglin Road, tel: 6424 4200
Canada: 11-01 One George Street, tel: 6854 5900

Above from far left: the little ones will have a splashing good time in Singapore; restored warehouse in Clarke Quay.

Crime and Safety
Singapore has one of the lowest crime rates in the world. Although it is generally a safe place, beware of pickpockets, especially in crowded areas. Place valuables in your hotel safe before heading out. It is generally safe for women to walk around alone, even at night.

Electricity

Electrical supply is on a 220–240 volt, 50 Hz system. Most hotels have transformers for 110–120 volt, 60 Hz appliances.

New Zealand: 15-06 Ngee Ann City Tower A, 391A Orchard Road, tel: 6235 9966.

USA: 27 Napier Road, tel: 6476 9100.

EMERGENCIES

Fire and ambulance: 995

Police: 999 (emergency), 1800-255 0000 (non-emergency)

Flight information: 1800-542 4422

Immigration & Checkpoints Authority: 6391 6100

STB Touristline: 1800-736 2000

Directory assistance: 100 (or 161 from public phone)

ETIQUETTE

Most good behaviour in Singapore is law-enforced; public signage is usually very good and there are clear signs explaining what to do and what not to do. Littering can cost you a fine of up to S$300 for first-time offenders; smoking in public places, including government offices, air-conditioned restaurants, cinemas and supermarkets, up to S$1,000; and using a mobile phone while driving is liable to a S$200 fine. You can now buy chewing gum – albeit only gum with 'therapeutic' value, for instance nicotine-laced gum to help smokers kick the habit.

There is no fine, thankfully, if you forget to remove your shoes before entering a mosque, Indian temple or an Asian home. When keeping company with Muslims and Hindus, neither eat with nor offer anything with your left hand.

F

FESTIVALS

Although the dates of ethnic festivals vary because they are based on the lunar calendar, most are confined to one or two specific months of the year. The only exception is the Muslim festival of Hari Raya Puasa, which advances by a month or so each year. The other major Muslim festival is Hari Raya Haji, which marks the sacrifices made by Muslims who make the pilgrimage to Mecca.

January/February

Lunar New Year is the most important festival for the Chinese. A colourful parade called **Chingay** is held, with cultures from all over the world celebrated. Also during this period is the Indian harvest festival of **Ponggal**. Then comes the Indian festival of **Thaipusam** where devotees go into a trance and perform acts of penance.

March/April

Good Friday, which precedes Easter, is observed at many Christian churches in Singapore. Also around this time the Chinese observe **Qing Ming** in remembrance of deceased ancestors and loved ones.

The **World Gourmet Summit** and **Singapore Film Festival** are also held during these months.

May/June/July

Vesak Day (May) commemorates Buddha's birth, enlightenment and

death. The **Dragon Boat Festival** (June) is held in remembrance of the poet Qu Yuan, who drowned himself in protest against political corruption in China. The annual **Singapore Arts Festival** (May/June) brings top-rate performers from around the world. The **Great Singapore Sale** (end May to mid July) is an island-wide shopping extravaganza. The **Singapore Food Festival** is held in July.

August/September

To celebrate **National Day** on 9 August, a parade and mass displays are held at the Marina Bay Floating Stadium; the evening ends with a fireworks display. The **Mooncake Festival** coincides with what is believed to be the year's brightest full moon during the eighth lunar month.

October/November/December

The most important Hindu festival **Deepavali** is in October/November. **ZoukOut**, an annual dance party is held at Sentosa's Siloso Beach. Orchard Road lights up for **Christmas**, and the year winds up with carols being sung in the streets and parties.

GAY/LESBIAN

Engaging in homosexual activity is an offence, but it does not mean it is non-existent. In general Singapore society is still fairly conservative when it comes to public displays of gay affection, and these actions are likely to draw stares. But that is about as much reaction as you will get as Singaporeans do not usually react aggressively to homosexuality. The unofficial gay hangout is Tanjong Pagar, where the majority of the gay bars are located. Singapore's gay websites are www.fridae.com and www.utopia-asia.com.

GOVERNMENT

Singapore has a unicameral government with general elections held once every five years. The People's Action Party (PAP) has been in power since independence in 1965. Lee Hsien Loong has been prime minister since 2004. The mainstays of the economy are manufacturing, finance and business services, commerce, transport and communications, tourism and construction. Singapore's GDP per capita (PPP) is US$43,867 (2010).

HEALTH

Singapore has no free medical care, so be sure you are covered by insurance. Most hotels have doctors on call. The local water off the tap is treated and safe for drinking. Strict control is exercised over the hygiene of food sold, from hawker stalls to hotels. If you require treatment, there are about 16 government and private hospitals as well as umpteen number of clinics for any eventuality. Singapore is fast gaining a reputation as a regional med-

Above from far left: there is always an event or festival taking place in Singapore, from beach parties to religious festivals like Thaipusam.

Measurements Most transactions in Singapore are metric, although the old imperial system is still occasionally used at the local produce markets.

Be Insured
Find out if your insurance policy has international coverage. Otherwise, be sure to buy travel insurance to cover hospitalisation and luggage loss.

ical hub par excellence; the number of foreigners seeking treatment here is high. Consultation fees start from about S$30 in a private practice.

Hospitals
Mount Elizabeth Hospital: 3 Mount Elizabeth; tel: 6737 2666; www.mount elizabeth.com.sg
Raffles Hospital: 585 North Bridge Road; tel: 6311 1111; www.raffles medical.com
Singapore General Hospital: Outram Road; tel: 6222 3322; www.sgh. com.sg

Pharmacies
These are open 9am–9pm. **Guardian**'s pharmacies have in-house pharmacists. It is wise to travel with your own prescriptions and medications.

Maps
Maps are available at the Changi Airport and the Singapore Tourism Board's office at Tourism Court, 1 Orchard Spring Lane; tel: 6736 6622, as well as at the Singapore Visitors Centre at the junction of Orchard and Cairnhill Roads.

I

INTERNET

To get online, head to an internet café; try **BlueChip Singapore Internet Café** (220 Orchard Road, 02-10 Midpoint Orchard Building; tel: 6100 7873; www.bluechipgroup.com.sg; daily 10am-10.30pm). **Wireless@SG** is a scheme that provides free wireless connection at selected hotspots. You will need a mobile device with Wi-fi facility and will need to register online with a service provider: **iCELL** (tel: 6309 4525; www.icellnetwork.com), **QMax** (tel: 6895 4833; www.qmax. com.sg) or **Singtel** (tel: 1610; www. singtel.com). Check the **Infocomm**

Development Authority website (www.ida.gov.sg) for the locations of all the hotspots.

L

LEFT LUGGAGE

These can be stored at the Changi Airport's Left Baggage counters at Terminal 1 (tel: 6214 0628, tel: 6214 0318), Terminal 2 (tel: 6214 0448, tel: 6214 1683) and Terminal 3 (tel: 6242 8936, tel: 6214 0672). Alternatively, check with any of the airport's information desks. Charges for the first 24 hours start at S$3.21 for cabin bags, S$4.28 for suitcases and S$8.56 for odd-sized items.

LOST PROPERTY

To lodge a police report, visit the nearest police station or call 1800-255 0000. For lost items on SMRT buses, call 1800-336 8900. For MRT trains, inform the station staff and for taxis, call the respective operators. For lost luggage at the airport, call 6511 0459 (Terminal 1 and 2), 6247 5714 (Terminal 3) or 9665 3046 (Budget Terminal).

M

MEDIA

Newspapers: *The Straits Times* and *The Business Times* are local English-language dailies with local and international news. *The New Paper*, a tabloid, is published in the morning and afternoon. *Today* is available free

at MRT stations. Foreign newspapers like the *International Herald Tribune*, *Financial Times* and *Asian Wall Street Journal* are available on the day of publication at major business hotels and large bookshops.

Radio: English-language channels are Gold FM (90.5 mhz), Symphony 92 FM (92.4 mhz), News Radio 938 (93.8 mhz), 987 FM (98.7 mhz); Class 95 FM (95 mhz); Radio 91.3 (91.3 mhz); and Power 98 (98.0 mhz). The BBC World Service is on 88.9 mhz.

Television: Local TV stations broadcast via the following channels: Channel 5 in English, Channel 8 and Channel U in Mandarin; Suria in Malay; Vasantham in Tamil; Okto shows kids programmes as well as documentaries and arts content and Channel NewsAsia broadcasts news and current affairs programmes. Cable is available through Starhub Cable TV, which operates 24 hours.

MONEY

The local currency consists of notes in $2, $5, $10, $50, $100, $500, $1,000 and $10,000 denominations. Coins are in denominations of 5, 10, 20, 50 cents and $1. Licensed moneychangers found in shopping malls offer the best rates. International charge and credit cards are widely accepted. Besides banks, there are ATMs in shopping centres, MRT stations, and at some major tourist attractions. Traveller's cheques can easily be encashed in most of the banks. Most large shops accept traveller's cheques in lieu of cash after conversion of the prevailing rate of exchange.

Tipping: Most hotel and restaurant bills come with a 10 percent service charge on top of a 7 percent Goods and Services Tax (GST). Tipping is not expected, but is appreciated in cases of special effort.

Taxes: A GST of 7 percent is charged on most purchases, which is refundable for visitors who make purchases from shops participating in the **Global Blue** and the **Premier Tax Free Scheme**, which display 'Tax Free Shopping' and 'Premier Tax Free' stickers respectively. The refund applies to purchases exceeding S$100. Show your passport to the retailer and fill out a voucher. Before departure, validate the voucher at the airport customs, then present it together with your purchased items at the Global Blue counter (tel: 6546 5089) or Premier Tax Free Scheme Counter (tel: 6546 4353). You can opt for cash or a refund back to your credit card.

P

PHOTOGRAPHY

Processing of both conventional and digital prints can be done within the hour at any of the photo stores found in malls and tourist areas. Singapore is one of the best places in Southeast Asia for the duty-free purchase of cameras, lenses and photography equipment. Sim Lim Square, Peninsula Plaza and Peninsula Hotel's shopping arcade have several specialist camera stores.

POSTAL SERVICES

Postal services are fast and efficient. Most hotels will handle mail for you or you may post letters and parcels at any post office. The **Singapore Post** branch at 1 Killiney Road is open Mon–Fri 9.30am–9pm, Sat 9.30am–4pm, and Sun and public 10.30am–4pm; the branch at the Changi Airport's Terminal 2 is open 6am–10.30pm daily. Call 1605 or check www.singpost.com.sg for more information about postal rates, express mail and other services, including its courier service called SpeedPost.

For other international courier services, check **DHL Express**' website at www.dhl.com.sg (or call 1800-285 8888), or **FedEx** at www.fedex.com.sg (or call 1800 743 2626).

PUBLIC HOLIDAYS

New Year's Day: 1 January
Chinese New Year: January/February
Good Friday: April
Labour Day: 1 May
Vesak Day: May
National Day: 9 August
Deepavali: October/November
Christmas Day: 25 December
Hari Raya Puasa: date varies
Hari Raya Haji: date varies

R

RELIGION

Buddhism and Taoism are most commonly practised by the Chinese, among whom about 20 percent are Christians. Malays are Muslim and Singaporeans of Indian descent are either Hindu, Sikh or Christian. The Eurasians and Peranakans are largely Christians, either Roman Catholic or Protestant.

S

SPORTS

Golf: Green fees range from S$40 for a nine-hole course on weekdays to S$400 for a full round at a championship course on weekends. Most golf and country clubs are open to visitors on weekdays only. Some clubs may ask you for a proficiency certificate.
Changi Golf Club, 20 Netheravon Road; tel: 6545 5133.
Raffles Country Club, 450 Jalan Ahmad Ibrahim; tel: 6861 7649.
Sentosa Golf Club, 27 Bukit Manis Road, Sentosa; tel: 6275 0090.
Tanah Merah Country Club, 25 Changi Coast Road; tel: 6542 3040.

Windsurfing: **SAFYC Sea Sports Centre**, 11 Changi Coast Walk; tel: 6546 5880; www.safyc.org.sg. Located near the Tanah Merah Ferry Terminal, this offers windsurfing, kayaking and laser sailing. There is a day fee of S$10 for use of the club. Rental fees for boats, kayaks and windsurf boards apply.

Waterskiing/Wakeboarding: **Extreme Sports**, Kallang Riverside Park; tel: 6334 8813; www.extreme.com.sg. You can both ski or wakeboard at Kallang River; it costs S$90 an hour on week-

days and S$120 on weekends, including equipment rental. Beginner lessons (4 sessions) cost S$150.

Cycling: Bicycles may be hired by the hour at East Coast Park's bike-hire kiosks and on Sentosa Island where there is a 5km (3-mile) track.

Horse Racing: Live races as well as live telecasts of Malaysian races can be enjoyed at **Singapore Turf Club** (tel: 6879 1000; www.turfclub.com.sg) in Kranji. Note: a strict dress code is enforced at the club. Singapore races are held on selected Friday nights and Saturday and Sunday afternoons.

TELEPHONES

The country code for Singapore is 65 (there are no area codes). To call overseas from Singapore, dial the international access code 001 or, for cheaper calls, either 013 or 019, followed by the relevant country code.

Mobile phone users with global roaming access should take note that the local network is GSM, common to most countries except Japan and the USA. To keep your costs down, buy a local SIM card from one of the three service providers: **Singtel** (tel: 1626 or 6738 0123), **M1** (tel: 1627 or 1800-843 8383) or **Starhub** (tel: 1633 or 6825 5000). These cards, which give you a local mobile number, cost a minimum of S$20 and can be topped up when the value

falls. All local mobile numbers begin with an '8' or '9'.

Coin-operated public phones are a rare sight in Singapore, given the high penetration levels of mobile phones. Post offices are your best bet; some phones here can be used for worldwide calls. For convenience, buy S$3, S$5, S$10, S$20 or S$50 phone cards for both local and overseas calls. Local calls cost 10 cents for every 3 minutes.

TOURIST INFORMATION

There's a wealth of free literature at the airport, hotels, shopping centres and tourist attractions. Your hotel concierge is also a good source of information.

The **Singapore Tourism Board** (24-hour infoline: 1800-736 2000; www. yoursingapore.com) operates several visitor centres. The most useful location is the **STB Visitors Centre** at the junction of Cairnhill Road and Orchard Road (daily 9.30am–10.30pm), just opposite the Somerset MRT station. Other STB Visitor Centres are found at Changi Airport, Bugis Street and ION Orchard.

TOURS

Trishaws: Although mainly used by tourist groups, you can hire a trishaw on your own. Just make sure you agree on the destination and fare before starting out. A tour of the city, lasting approximately 30 minutes, will cost S$39. Contact **Trishaw Uncle** (tel: 9012 1233; www.trishawuncle.com.sg) for more information.

Above from far left: rollerblading at the East Coast Park; devotees at a Hindu temple.

Smoking
Smoking is not allowed at all enclosed public places like restaurants, museums, theatres, cinemas, shopping malls and government offices – in short almost everywhere in Singapore! The penalty for a smoking offence is S$1,000. Some restaurants have alfresco sections with designated smoking areas, and many bars and clubs have enclosed rooms reserved for smokers. Several hotels are now fully smoke-free but most still have smoking rooms or entire floors.

Toilets

Singapore's toilets are some of the cleanest in the world. In shopping malls, there are toilets on every floor and in tourist attractions there are ample toilets for the convenience of visitors. The majority of the toilets are very well-maintained except for some old buildings and hawker centres. Note: you may have to pay a 20-cent fee to enter some toilets in Singapore.

SIA Hop-On: This is a tourist bus service that operates unlimited rides to the various attractions in the city from 9am to 7.30pm daily. It stops at major hotels, shopping malls and landmarks. Contact **SH Tours** (tel: 6734 9923; www.asiatours.com.sg) for information.

HiPPO City Tours: You can purchase a one- or two-day **Singapore Sightseeing Pass** from the **DUCK & HiPPO Group** (tel: 6338 6877; www.ducktours.com.sg). With this pass, you have unlimited access to five City HiPPOtours; each tour travels a themed route and takes you to key districts and attractions around the island. The tours come with live commentary and you have the option of hopping on and off at any time and anywhere. The company also offers a two-day **Singapore Pass**, which combines 15 tours and attractions, including the popular DUCKtours.

Boats: A cruise on a bumboat is a novel way of taking in the sights along the Singapore River. Operated by **Singapore River Cruises** (tel: 6336 6111; www.rivercruise.com.sg), the boats ply two routes: the 30-minute round trip costs S$15 and the longer 45-minute round trip costs S$20. Tickets can be purchased at one of the river's nine jetties: Merlion Park, Fullerton Hotel, Boat Quay, Raffles' Landing Site, Riverside Point, Liang Court, Merchant Loop, Roberston Quay and Grand Copthorne Waterfront.

Themed Tours

RMG Tours (tel: 6220 8722), **Singapore Sightseeing** (tel: 6336 9011), **SH Tours** (tel: 6734 9923) and **Holiday Tours** (tel: 6738 2622) operate half- and full-day tours. Apart from the usual tours, these companies also operate themed tours that focus on cuisine, *feng shui* (Chinese geomancy), colonial history and other aspects of Singapore.

Journeys' Original Singapore Walks (tel: 6325 1631; www.singaporewalks.com) has walking tours to places like Little India, Chinatown, Kampong Glam and the Civic District. Its Changi Museum War Trails is a coach tour that focuses on World War II Singapore.

TRANSPORT

Getting There

By Air: Changi Airport (www.changiairport.com; tel: 1800-542 4422 for flight information; tel: 6542 9727 (Terminal 1), 6542 9792 (Terminal 2), 6307 8555 (Terminal 3), 6412 7500 (Budget Terminal) for customer service) is consistently polled the world's best airport by travellers and businessmen. There are work spaces for laptops, business centres, an airport hotel, gym, and more; improvements and new facilities are constantly being added. There are four terminals – Terminal 1 (T1), Terminal 2 (T2), Terminal 3 (T3) and the Budget Terminal.

All three terminals offer a large assortment of duty-free shops, food outlets, bars and entertainment options. Passengers can also shuttle between T1,

T2 and T3 by the **Sky Train** service (daily 5am–2.30am). The Budget Terminal's (BT) offerings are basic, but its passengers can easily connect to T2 and its amenities using the **BT Shuttle Service**, available 24 hours daily.

Changi Airport is linked directly to 200 cities in 60 countries, with 100 airlines operating over 5,400 flights a week. The award-winning **Singapore Airlines** (www.singaporeair.com) flies to 93 destinations in 38 countries and its sister airline **SilkAir** (www.silkair.com) serves 34 destinations in Asia.

By Sea: Most visitors on a cruise arrive at the **Singapore Cruise Centre** (tel: 6513 2200; www.singaporecruise.com) located at the HarbourFront Centre. Singapore-based cruise liners sail to various countries in the region and also offer one-way cruise options. Contact **Star Cruises** (tel: 6226 1168; www.starcruises.com) for more information.

Tanah Merah Ferry Terminal (tel: 6545 2048), located near Changi Airport, has ferry services to Bintan and Batam islands in Indonesia and also to Tioman island in Malaysia.

By Road: Singapore is accessible by road from Ipoh and Kuala Lumpur on the west coast, and Kota Bharu on the east. It takes about 5 hours to drive from Kuala Lumpur (KL) via the North-South Highway. Travelling via Johor Bahru, entry into Singapore is either through the Woodlands Check point in the north of Singapore or the Tuas Second Link in the west. Several private bus companies and travel agents in Singapore operate air-conditioned bus services to Malaysia and southern Thailand. **Transtar Travel** at 01-15 Golden Mile Complex, 5001 Beach Road, has frequent daily departures and tickets can be booked online (tel: 6299 9009; www.transtar.com.sg).

By Rail: A railway line links Singapore to KL, Butterworth and Bangkok, as well as to Tumpat, near Kota Bharu. Enquire at the **Woodlands Train Checkpoint** (tel: 6767 5722; www.ica.gov.sg.

The **Eastern & Orient Express** has a luxury train that travels the 1,900km (1,200-mile) route linking Bangkok, KL and Singapore (tel: 6395 0678; www.orient-express.com).

Getting Around

From the airport: There are several easy ways of getting to town from the airport.

The taxi stands at the Changi Airport are well organised. The 20-minute trip (barring peak-hour traffic) to the city on the East Coast Parkway (ECP) costs about S\$25, including surcharges.

If you wish to travel in style, book a premium Limousine Taxi at a flat rate of S\$45 per one-way trip (6am–midnight) and S\$55 (midnight–6am). For larger groups, a 7-seater Maxicab costs a flat rate of S\$50 per one-way trip to any destination (no midnight surcharge).

The Airport Shuttle operates air-conditioned 9-seater coaches which serve all major hotels except those in Changi and Sentosa. Buy tickets at the Airport Shutttle Counter of all ter-

minals. Tickets cost S$9 (adult) and S$6 (child), and the bus departs every 15 minutes from 6am–midnight, and 30 minutes from midnight to 6am.

The train ride from the airport to the City Hall MRT station downtown, with a transfer at the Tanah Merah MRT station takes about 30 minutes. The train ticket costs S$1.90.

The airport is also served by air-conditioned public buses, the stands for which are located in the basements of T1, 2 and 3. Bus no. 36 takes you direct to the city. The ticket costs below S$2 and exact change is required.

Taxis: The easiest way to see Singapore is by taxi. There are more than 23,000 taxis plying the roads and most drivers speak or understand English. Within the CBD (and Orchard Road), taxis must be boarded and alighted at taxi stands or on side roads. Elsewhere, simply flag one down on the street. During peak hours, or when it is raining, booking a taxi is the best option. Call tel: 6342 5222, or the individual taxi companies: **Comfort/CityCab** (tel: 6552 1111), or **SMRT** (tel: 6555 8888). Flag-down fare starts from S$2.80 to S$3.20 for the first kilometre, depending on the type of taxi you get. Most taxis accept credit cards.

A slew of surcharges apply: advance bookings, Electronic Road Pricing (ERP), midnight (midnight–6am), extra baggage, peak-hour; airport surcharge for taxis that depart from the airport.
Cars: **Avis** (tel: 6737 1668) and **Hertz** (tel: 1800-734 4646) offer both self-drive and chauffeur-driven cars. You will need an international driver's license. Driving is on the left and seat belts are compulsory. Also, you must understand the **Electronic Road Pricing** (ERP) system before you drive. During peak hours, the ERP scheme controls traffic flow into the Central Business District and on major expressways. There is a scale of charges applicable to different periods and vehicle types. Charges are indicated on electronic boards just before an ERP gantry. When you drive through an ERP gantry, it will automatically deduct the correct fee from the cash card inserted into a special gadget in your car. Pre-paid cash cards are available at post offices or petrol stations; most car rental companies will also sell you one.

Buses: Efficient bus services operated by **SBS Transit** and **SMRT** cover most of the island and operate from 6am–midnight. Fares are S$0.80 to S$1.50 for non-air-conditioned buses and S$0.90 to S$1.80 for air-conditioned buses.

Be sure to have the exact fare as bus drivers do not give change. For convenience, buy a S$15 **ez-link card** which is inclusive of S$5 card cost (non-refundable), S$3 travel deposit and S$7 stored value. This allows cashless payment on all public buses and the MRT. By using the ez-link card, commuters can also enjoy lower fares and rebates when transferring between trains and buses.

Tap your e-z link card on the electronic reader located at the bus entrance (or turnstile at the MRT sta-

Singapore's weather is hot and humid year round. Light, cottonwear or shorts and t-shirts are best when doing walking tours. Comfortable walking shoes, sandals and sunglasses are useful for getting around. Umbrellas and raincoats are always handy as downpours are unpredictable. A light cardigan or shawl is sometimes required in air-conditioned indoors. Note that mosques require that arms and legs be fully covered (by long-sleeved shirts, long pants and long skirts or sarongs) to enter. Sikh temples require visitors to wear a head covering, as do synagogues for males.

tion), which then automatically deducts the maximum fare. When alighting from the bus or disembarking from the train, tap the card again on the reader at the exit, and the unused fare portion will be credited back into the card.

Ez-link cards are sold at Transitlink offices at all MRT stations and bus interchanges. When the value of your card runs low, you can top it up at these same offices. For information on ez link cards and concession passes, visit www.transitlink.com.sg.

An alternative is the **Singapore Tourist Pass** (www.thesingaporetourist pass.com), which gives visitors unlimited rides on Singapore's MRT, LRT and bus services. 1-day (S$8), 2-day (S$16) and 3-day (S$24) tickets are available (with a S$10 refundable deposit) and can be bought at selected MRT stations and the Singapore Visitors Centre at Orchard Road. This pass comes with a free copy of the **'Travel with Ease – Public Transport Guide for Tourists'** guide, which contains useful information on the various modes of public transport and gives travel directions to various sights and attractions. The guide is available free at Singapore Visitors Centres and selected MRT stations.

MRT: The efficiency of the city's metro system, known as the **Mass Rapid Transit** (MRT) (www.smrt.com.sg) draws the envy of commuters everywhere. Altogether, there are 78 stations on the North-East Line, East-West and North-South and Circle lines. Trains operate around 5.15am–

12.49am and fares are S$0.90–1.90. Trains run at intervals of 2–8 minutes depending on the time of travel. The price of a single-trip ticket dispensed by ticket machines include a S$1 deposit. This is refunded by the ticket machine at the end of your trip. This can be a bother, so if you plan to use buses and the MRT for several trips, buy a stored-value **ez-link card** or the **Singapore Tourist Pass**. Tap your card on the electronic readers at the start and end of your trip as you do on buses.

V

VISAS AND PASSPORTS

Visa requirements can vary, so check with a Singapore embassy or consular office in your home country. Most visitors are given a 30-day social visit pass on arrival. Application for renewals can be made online or at the **Immigration & Checkpoints Authority** (ICA), 10 Kallang Road. For details, call the hotline: 6391 6100; www.ica.gov.sg.

W

WEBSITES

www.yoursingapore.com – Singapore Tourism Board's site providing general tourist information.
www.sg – official government site with facts and figures on Singapore.
www.makansutra.com – informative site detailing the best hawker fare.
www.timeoutsingapore.com – listings of events, nightspots and restaurants.

Above from far left: Electronic Road Pricing gantry; Singapore has an efficient public bus system.

Civic District

Carlton

76 Bras Basah Road; tel: 6338 8333; www.carlton.com.sg; $$

This business-class hotel sits on a prime spot across from Chijmes and the Raffles Hotel. Choose from rooms in the Main Tower, Executive Wing or Premier Wing. Award-winning Cantonese restaurant and a 24-hour café on site. A 5-minute walk to the City Hall MRT station.

Fairmont Singapore

80 Bras Basah Road; tel: 6339 7777; www.fairmont.com/singapore; $$$$

Fairmont has 769 luxurious guest rooms and suites, with private balconies overlooking panoramic views of the harbour or the cityscape. The hotel also offers a long list of amenities and excellent restaurants, including Szechuan Court and Inagiku. Its Willow Stream Spa is perfect for rejuvenating spa treatments. The City Hall MRT station is literally at its doorstep.

Hangout@Mt.Emily

10A Upper Wilkie Road; tel: 6438 5588; www.hangouthotels.com; $$

This funky backpacker's lodging is about a 10-minute walk from the Dhoby Ghaut MRT station. Rooms are clean but small and with few frills. A great place to meet other travellers.

Hotel Fort Canning

11 Canning Walk; tel: 6559 6770; www.hfcsingapore.com; $$-$$$

This colonial building was the British Far East Command Headquarters during World War II. Rooms are individually styled and there's also a gym, pool and Thailand's renowned Thann Spa. Free internet access for all guests.

Naumi

41 Seah Street; tel: 6403 6000; www.naumihotel.com; $$$

A chic 40-room boutique hotel, the Naumi offers plush designer comfort, a 50-in plasma TV, kitchenette and Wi-fi connectivity. An inviting rooftop infinity pool overlooks the city's skyline. The hotel's sixth floor is for ladies only. The City Hall MRT station is a convenient 5-minute walk away.

Raffles

1 Beach Road; tel: 6337 1886; www.raffleshotel.com; $$$$

The Grand Dame of historical hotels. Guests stay in suites and are cocooned in a private, genteel world where one is greeted by name and treads on wooden floors lined with antique rugs while gazing at museum-quality art pieces. The private pool is open 24 hours and bathrooms are designed for absolute indulgence. Across the road is the City Hall MRT station.

Price for a double room for one night without breakfast (not including the 10 per cent service charge and 7 per cent goods and services tax, except where noted):

$$$$	over S$500
$$$	S$350–500
$$	S$150–350
$	below S$150

Swissôtel The Stamford

2 Stamford Road; tel: 6338 8585; www.swissotel.com; $$$

Once the world's tallest hotel until it was supplanted in 1999, this hotel sits above the City Hall MRT station and is practically part of a large shopping centre complex. Business centre, convention centre and a huge number of restaurants and bars (including the rooftop Equinox complex), plus a luxurious spa and a well-equipped fitness centre.

Marina Bay

Conrad Centennial

2 Temasek Boulevard; tel: 6334 8880; www.conradhotels.com; $$$$

This five-star has spacious and luxurious rooms with picturesque views of Marina Bay. Excellent choice for business travellers with its wide range of facilities and fine restaurants such as Golden Peony and Oscar's. The service staff are highly efficient. Convenient location for shopping, and only five minutes' walk to the Promenade MRT station.

The Fullerton

1 Fullerton Square; tel: 6733 8388; www.fullertonhotel.com; $$$$

Formerly the General Post Office, this historical jewel is now a luxury hotel. The colonnaded exterior gives way to a contemporary chic interior filled with Art Deco furniture. Amazing views from the 400 rooms and suites which either overlook the sunlit atrium courtyard, or have balconies that open out to panoramas of the city skyline, river promenade or Marina Bay. Raffles Place MRT station is 5 minutes away.

Mandarin Oriental

5 Raffles Avenue; tel: 6338 0066; www.mandarinoriental.com; $$$$

Its plush rooms have floor-to-ceiling windows that overlook the city. Well known for its eateries – Morton of Chicago steakhouse, Cherry Garden Cantonese restaurant and the poolside Mediterranean-style Dolce Vita restaurant. The Promenade MRT station is 5 minutes' walk away.

Marina Bay Sands

10 Bayfront Avenue; tel: 6688 8888; www.marinabaysands.com; $$$

Located in the massive Marina Bay Sands integrated resort, this hotel overlooks the city centre and bay area. Pick from 18 types of rooms, such as Atrium rooms and Horizon rooms. Among the many facilities in the complex are a stunning infinity pool, casino, shops as well as trendy bars and clubs.

Marina Mandarin

6 Raffles Boulevard; tel: 6845 1000; www.meritushotels.com; $$$

Apart from its spectacular atrium rising through 21 storeys, all rooms offer breathtaking views of Marina Bay, while premier rooms and suites are equipped with plasma TVs. The hotel's fine restaurants include Peach Blossoms for Chinese food and Ristorante Bologna for Italian cuisine. Only a short walk to the Esplanade MRT station.

Pan Pacific Singapore

7 Raffles Boulevard; tel: 6336 8111; www.panpacific.com/singapore; $$$

Above from far left: top-notch service staff from the legendary Raffles Hotel; executive club room at Marina Mandarin.

John Portman

There are several five-star hotels in Singapore that are designed by John Portman, the renowned American architect. They are Marina Mandarin, Mandarin Oriental and Pan Pacific, all located in the prime Marina Bay area and linked to Marina Square shopping mall. Portman also designed The Regent near Orchard Road.

Extra Charges

When booking directly with the hotel, always ask if they have promotional rates and if breakfast is included in the rate. And be aware that the standard 10 percent service charge and 7 percent Goods and Services Tax (GST) will add significantly to the final rate.

This hotel's 778 rooms and suites are contemporary and elegant, replete with beautiful views of the city or Marina Bay. It is the first hotel in Singapore to offer Wi-fi-operated mini-bars. Fine dining Indian, Japanese and Chinese cuisines are offered at its restaurants. The Promenade MRT station is a short walk away.

Ritz-Carlton Millenia

7 Raffles Avenue; tel: 6337 8888; www.ritzcarlton.com/hotels/singapore; $$$$

The sheer luxury hits you the moment you step into the foyer, with its contemporary design and marble-clad spaces studded with Dale Chihuly glass sculptures. Rooms are equally luxe but the pièce de résistance must surely be the oversized bathrooms with huge picture windows framing the large bathtubs. A less than five-minute walk to the Promenade MRT station.

Singapore River

Gallery

1 Nanson Road; tel: 6849 8686; www.galleryhotel.com.sg; $$-$$$

Located in the Robertson Quay district, this 'design hotel' features postmodern architecture and lively, if a bit strange, decor and a variety of room sizes. The unique glass-sided pool is a definite highlight.

Grand Copthorne Waterfront

392 Havelock Road; tel: 6733 0880; www.grandcopthorne.com.sg; $$-$$$$

The rooms are nicely appointed and outfitted with wireless technology and Internet phones. Also offers a long-stay option; La Residenza on the fifth and sixth floors comprises 24 luxurious one- or two-bedroom units which come with kitchenettes.

Chinatown

Hotel 1929

50 Keong Saik Road; tel: 6347 1929; www.hotel1929.com; $$

Just outside the hubbub of Chinatown, this boutique property combines a mix of old-world Singapore architecture and nouveau chic style. No two rooms are the same and many are embellished with unique furniture from the owner's private collection. Its restaurant, Ember, which serves modern cuisine with an Asian twist has a strong following.

Link

50 Tiong Bahru Road; tel: 6622 8585; www.linkhotel.com.sg; $$

Billed as the biggest boutique hotel in Singapore, it features a contemporary design based on multicultural themes: Chinese, Indian and Malay. The hotel's prewar buildings, the Lotus and

Price for a double room for one night without breakfast (not including the 10 per cent service charge and 7 per cent goods and services tax, except where noted):

$$$$	over S$500
$$$	S$350–500
$$	S$150–350
$	below S$150

Orchid blocks, are connected by a unique bridge that spans across the bustling Tiong Bahru Road.

New Majestic
31–37 Bukit Pasoh Road, tel. 6511 4700; www.newmajestichotel.com; $$$

Local artists and designers had a hand in the interiors of the stylish and eclectic 30-room New Majestic. Each room has its own quirky character and features vibrant wall murals and claw-footed bathtubs. A highlight is its rooftop pool with glass portholes through which one can have a peek of what diners are eating at the New Majestic restaurant just below. Only a 2-minute walk to the Outram Park MRT station.

The Scarlet
33 Erskine Road; tel: 6511 3333; www.thescarlethotel.com; $$

Located near Ann Siang Hill and Club Street, this 80-room boutique hotel is full of character. Its unabashedly gaudy interior is decked out in bold colours, and its five custom-designed suites each showcase a different personality. There is a gym, an open air jacuzzi and a chic roof-top alfresco bar and restaurant overlooking Chinatown. The Chinatown MRT station is a 10-minute walk away.

Orchard Road

Four Seasons
190 Orchard Boulevard; tel: 6734 1110; www.fourseasons.com/singapore; $$$$

An intimate and elegant property with a marbled foyer, plush furnishings and exquisite artworks – about 1,500 Asian and international art pieces are on display. All rooms feature custom-designed beds, DVD and CD players with iPod docks, marble bathrooms with double vanity basins, deep-soaking tubs and luxuries such as Italian cotton bathrobes and Japanese yukatas. Only a 5-minute walk to the Orchard MRT station.

Goodwood Park
22 Scotts Road; tel: 6737 7411; www.goodwoodparkhotel.com.sg; $$$

This grand and graceful landmark exudes a strong colonial-era charm, with landscaped gardens that add a touch of serenity to the bustle of Orchard Road. It has 233 tastefully appointed rooms and suites complete with modern amenities, two outdoor swimming pools, a gym and eight excellent dining outlets. The Orchard MRT station is a 3-minute walk away.

Grand Hyatt
10 Scotts Road; tel: 6738 1234; www.singapore.grand.hyatt.com; $$$$

A stone's throw from the Orchard MRT station, the Grand Hyatt impresses with its minimalist, almost stark decor and excellent service. The Grand Wing rooms are particularly lavish with soft linens and Bang & Olufsen sound systems. Dine at mezza9 where Sunday champagne brunch is a must.

Grand Park Orchard
270 Orchard Road; tel: 6603 8888; www.parkhotelgroup.com/gpor/; $$-$$$

Bookings
An online hotel reservation system managed by the Singapore Hotel Association (SHA) can help you with last-minute bookings (www.stayinsingapore.com). You can select from 21,000 rooms of different categories and rates from over 50 hotels. The system provides real-time reservation with instant confirmation. SHA also has reservation counters at Changi Airport's Terminals 1, 2, 3 and the Budget Terminal arrival halls to assist you with bookings.

The hotel's location right in the middle of Orchard Road is highly convenient for shopaholics. The striking 'herringbone' design featured on its exterior glass facade is echoed throughout the hotel including the stylishly designed rooms.

Marriott

320 Orchard Road; tel: 6735 5800; www.singaporemarriott.com; $$$

The pagoda-roofed hotel at the corner of Scotts and Orchard roads is a well-known landmark with the Orchard MRT station at its doorstep. Its location is perfect for shopping and nightlife. Popular alfresco café, Cantonese restaurant and a poolside grill. The famous Tangs department store shares the same building.

Meritus Mandarin Singapore

333 Orchard Road; tel: 6737 4411; www.mandarin-singapore.com; $$$

Fantastic location on Orchard Road and 1,200 tastefully refurbished rooms that feature in-room amenities like flatscreen TVs, mini hi-fi systems and other bells and whistles. Premier rooms are equipped with sleek massage armchairs – perfect after a day's shopping. Two MRT stations (Orchard and Somerset) are within walking distance.

Royal Plaza on Scotts

25 Scotts Road; tel: 6737 7966; www.royalplaza.com.sg; $$$

Located on Scotts Road (near Orchard Road MRT station), this hotel offers tastefully decorated contemporary rooms with generous work spaces and complimentary in-room minibar, which is replenished daily. It is the first smoke-free business hotel in Singapore. Its lobby café, Carousel, features an international buffet spread and a gourmet deli filled with sweet treats.

St Regis

29 Tanglin Road; tel: 6506 6888; www.stregis.com; $$$$

St Regis brings its trademark style to a prime spot on Orchard Road. The design and furnishings are a bit over the top, but no one can fault its stupendous range of facilities: pool-side Italian restaurant, fine dining Cantonese, French Brasserie, spa, swimming pool, business centre, private butlers for every room and a fleet of Bentleys to chauffeur guests around. The Orchard Road MRT station is a good 10-minute walk away.

Little India

Moon @ 23 Dickson

23 Dickson Road; tel: 6827 6666; www.moon.com.sg; $

This is a no-fuss boutique hotel that's trendy, compact and comfortable. It's

---

Price for a double room for one night without breakfast (not including the 10 per cent service charge and 7 per cent goods and services tax, except where noted):

$$$$	over S$500
$$$	S$350–500
$$	S$150–350
$	below S$150

also close to Bugis MRT station, thus making it very convenient to get to any part of the city.

Parkroyal on Kitchener Road

181 Kitchener Road, tel: 6428 3000; www.parkroyalhotels.com; $$
Excellent-value hotel near Serangoon Road, next to the Farrer Park MRT station and opposite the 24-hour Mustafa Centre. Rooms are spacious and feature modern comforts. Facilities include a café serving Asian and Western food, Cantonese restaurant, executive floors, fitness centre and swimming pool.

Wanderlust Hotel

2 Dickson Road; tel: 6396 3322; wanderlusthotel.com; $$
Housed in an old school built in the 1920s, the concept of this hotel is incredibly unique. Each of the four levels was designed by award-winning local design agencies. The rooms are quirky and fun, albeit rather small. Its restaurant Cocotte dishes up hearty French fare.

Sentosa

Amara Sanctuary Resort

1 Larkhill Road; tel: 6825 3888; sentosa.amarahotels.com; $$$
This stylish resort is set amid lush tropical greenery and features a tasteful blend of colonial architecture and contemporary design. Formerly British military barracks, the courtyard suites have been transformed into romantic accommodation with outdoor jacuzzis in private gardens. Ten luxurious villas have private plunge pools and personal

butler service. All rooms offer free local calls and broadband Internet access.

Hard Rock Hotel Singapore

8 Sentosa Gateway, Sentosa Island; tel: 6577 8899; www.hardrockhotel singapore.com; $$-$$$
Live it up like a rock star and get the legendary entertainment experience. Located within the Resorts World Sentosa integrated resort, you can visit Universal Studios and explore the rest of the island during your stay.

The Sentosa Resort & Spa

2 Bukit Manis Road, tel: 6275 0331; www.thesentosa.com; $$$
Stunning resort-style hotel located on a forested hill. Features both hotel-style rooms and suites as well as villas with private pools. Linked by a path directly to the beach. You may just want to park yourself at this idyllic retreat and not venture into the city. Be sure to book a massage at its adjacent Spa Botanica, set in lush gardens.

Shangri-La's Rasa Sentosa Resort

101 Siloso Road; tel: 6275 0100; www.shangri-la.com; $$$-$$$$
Thanks to an S$80 million makeover, this resort now has upgraded guestrooms and facilities. Not the most convenient place to stay for easy access to the city, but the resort offers extensive recreational activities, from sailing to cycling. Restaurants here include Silver Shell Café, Trapizza and Barnacles serving Mediterranean dishes and Asian-inspired specialities.

Above from far left: the contemporary Royal Plaza on Scotts; The Sentosa Resort & Spa's family suite.

Hotel Boom
Since the opening of the two integrated resorts in Singapore – at Sentosa and Marina Bay – there are even more plush hotels on the island now. Resorts World Sentosa (www. rwsentosa.com) has six new hotels – Crockfords Tower, Hotel Michael, Hard Rock Hotel, Festive Hotel, Equarius Hotel and Spa Villas. Marina Bay Sands Hotel (www.marina baysands.com) offers stunning views of the city skyline or the sea, regardless of which of the 18 types of rooms you book yourself into.

Civic District

Italian
Garibaldi

01-02, 36 Purvis Street; tel: 6837 1468; www.garibaldi.com.sg; daily noon-3pm, 6.30-11pm; $$$$

Garibaldi is synonymous with Italian fine dining in the city. Helmed by well-known Chef Roberto Galetti, the kitchen uses only the best seasonal ingredients from Italy. His specialities include angel hair pasta with spiny lobster and a variety of robust risottos.

Japanese
Inagiku

3/F, Fairmont Singapore, 80 Bras Basah Road; tel: 6431 6156; www.fairmont.com/singapore; daily noon–2.30pm and 6.30–10.30pm; $$$$

Dine on beautifully executed Japanese creations made of premium ingredients air-flown from Japan. The chefs pair time-honoured traditions with contemporary techniques.

Peranakan
True Blue

47/49 Armenian Street; tel: 6440 0449; www.truebluecuisine.com; Tue–Sat 11.30am–2.30pm and 6–9.30pm; $$$

Located close to the Peranakan Museum, this eatery is adorned with the owner Benjamin Seck's personal collection of Peranakan antiques and artefacts. The dishes are just as impressive, but portions are small. Try the spicy beef *rendang* and *ayam buah keluak* (chicken stewed with black nuts) – all lovingly prepared by Benjamin's mother, Daisy.

Thai
Yhingthai Palace

36 Purvis Street; tel: 6337 1161; daily 11.30am–2pm and 6.30–10pm; $$

This restaurant serves delightfully robust Thai cuisine. Must-tries include the squid salad, three-flavoured fried fish, string beans with shrimp, and for dessert, mango with sticky rice.

Marina Bay

DB Bistro Moderne

10 Bayfront Avenue, #B1-48 The Shoppes at Marina Bay Sands; tel: 6688 8525; Mon–Fri noon–2.30pm, Mon–Sun 5.30–10.30pm, Sat–Sun 11am–2.30pm; $$$$

Located across the theatre, this contemporary American French bistro helmed by celebrity chef Daniel Boulud serves robust French fare created with flair. Its coq au vin and famous DB burger are must-tries. Brunch is served on weekends and a pre-theatre menu is available from 5.30pm to 7pm daily.

My Humble House

02-27 Esplanade Mall; tel: 6423 1881; www.tunglok.com; daily 11.45am–3pm and 10.30–11pm; $$$$

This restaurant is known for its eye-popping creative decor. Plonk yourself on the oversized seats and enjoy the lovely water views while waiting for the artistically plated Chinese dishes to be served. Mainstays are the wok-grilled pork ribs in champagne reduction and double-boiled seafood soup in coconut.

Pizzeria Mozza

10 Bayfront Avenue, #B1-42/46 The Shoppes at Marina Bay Sands; tel: 6688 8868; www.pizzeriamozza.com; daily noon-midnight; $$-$$$

Pizzeria Mozza (adjacent to the finer Osteria Mozza) is celebrity chef Mario Batali's first venture into Asia. Mirroring his restaurant in California, this pizza joint filled with blaring rock music is lively and casual. There are two wood-burning ovens that churn out the most delicious pizzas in town.

Waku Ghin

Marina Bay Sands, 10 Bayfront Avenue, Level 2 Casino; tel: 6688 8507; www.wakughin.com; daily 6.30–10.30pm; $$$$

This is renowned chef Tetsuya Wakuda's first restaurant outside of Sydney. Enjoy top-notch European cuisine with Japanese influence using the freshest seasonal ingredients. The experience is highly personalised as you can talk to the chefs and watch them prepare your degustation meal right in front of you.

Indian
Rang Mahal

3/F, Pan Pacific Hotel, 7 Raffles Boulevard; tel: 6333 1788; www. rangmahal.com.sg; Sun–Fri noon–2.30pm, daily 6.30–10.30pm; $$$$

This elegant restaurant has been serving top-class Indian cuisine from the northern, southern and coastal regions since 1971. Dine on innovative fare like tandoori oyster, and lamb shank in saffron- and cardamom-flavoured cashew gravy. Chefs prepare *phulka* (freshly puffed wheat bread) at your table by placing them over a small stove until the bread balloons.

French
Le Saint Julien

02-01, 3 Fullerton Road; tel: 6534 5947; www.saintjulien.com.sg; Mon–Fri noon–2pm and Mon–Sat 6.30–10pm; $$$$

Frenchman Julien Bompard's résumé includes Michelin-starred restaurants. Now the commander of his own place, Bompard does what he does best: classical French cuisine complemented by a fine French wine list – in a quaint old boat house by the waterfront.

Saint Pierre

01-01 Central Mall, 3 Magazine Road; tel: 6438 0887; www.saint pierre.com.sg; Mon–Fri noon–3pm, Mon–Sat 7pm–midnight; $$$$

This restaurant is extremely popular and reservations are a must. Owned by Belgian Emmanuel Stroobant, it features half a dozen foie gras dishes. Favourites include pan-fried foie gras with caramelised green apple, braised black cod with white miso and Grandma Stroobant's flourless chocolate cake.

Price guide for a meal for one (excluding drinks and taxes):	
$$$$	over S$50
$$$	S$30–50
$$	S$10–30
$	below S$10

Above from far left: exquisite decor at True Blue; savoury bouchée at Rang Mahal; tempura at Inagiku ; private room at the fine-dining Inagiku.

Restaurant Guides
For a guide to the best restaurants in Singapore, pick up *Singapore Tatler's Singapore's Best Restaurants* or the *Miele Guide*, which is a comprehensive guide to the best restaurants in Asia's major cities.

Organic Eats

Organic food does not figure much on Singaporean dining tables due to its high cost, but there are a handful of places where you can enjoy healthy organic cuisine. For instance, Holland Village's Bunalun (01-70, 43 Chip Bee Gardens, Jalan Merah Saga, tel: 6472 0870) whips up delicious gourmet meals, salads and pastries. The retail section stocks a good range of organic produce, from spices and herbs to dried fruits and pastas. The Garden (Sentosa Resort and Spa, 2 Bukit Manis Road, Sentosa, tel: 6371 1130) next to Spa Botanica uses ingredients that are specially sourced from organic or bio-dynamic farms, where possible.

Fusion
Coriander Leaf
02-03 Clarke Quay, River Valley Road; tel: 6732 3354; www.corianderleaf. com; Mon–Fri noon–2pm and 6.30–10pm, Sat 6.30–10.30pm; $$$$
This atmospheric restaurant overlooking the river showcases a brilliant pan-Asian menu given a Western spin. Try the mezze (various dips with grilled chicken wings and spinach triangles) and spiced-rubbed rack of lamb. Delicious sides include various naan breads and coriander-spiked rice.

International
Ellenborough Market Café
Swissotel Merchant Court Hotel, 20 Merchant Road; tel: 6239 1848; daily noon–2.30pm and 6.30–10pm, high tea 3.30–5.30pm; $$$
Overlooking the Singapore River, this restaurant is especially popular among locals who love the buffet spread of international and local favourites. Dine on *nonya dishes*, chicken curry, satay, *laksa*, sushi and sashimi, then finish off with a plethora of desserts like coconut-based *cendol*, *pandan* crème brûlée, rum and raisin bread pudding and assorted *nonya* cakes.

Modern Australian
Moomba
52 Circular Road; tel: 6438 0141; www.themoomba.com; Mon–Fri 11am–2.30pm, Mon–Sat 6.30–10pm; $$$$
The city's first Australian restaurant is still among the best. Expect an extensive collection of boutique Australian wines and creative contemporary Australian cuisine. Its squid ink risotto is one of the best in town.

Chinatown

Spring Court
52-56 Upper Cross Street; tel: 6449 5030; www.springcourt.com.sg; daily 11am–2.30pm, 6–10.30pm; $$$
Established in 1929, this successful family-run restaurant in Chinatown is considered one of the oldest Cantonese restaurants in Singapore. Classics include crisp roast chicken, popiah (spring rolls) and golden cereal prawns. *Dim sum* is available for lunch.

Modern Chinese
Majestic Restaurant
1/F, New Majestic Hotel, 31-37 Bukit Pasoh Road; tel: 6511 4718; 11.45am–3pm, 6.30–11pm; $$$$
This stylish restaurant is reknowned for its individually plated modern Cantonese cuisine such as the combination of wasabi prawn, Peking duck and pan-seared foie gras or the grilled rack of lamb with Chinese honey. Diners get a view of the swimmers in the pool above through portholes in the ceiling.

Price guide for a meal for one (excluding drinks and taxes):	
$$$$	over S$50
$$$	S$30–50
$$	S$10–30
$	below S$10

Modern Italian

Buko Nero

126 Tanjong Pagar Road; tel: 6324 6225, Fri–Sat noon–2pm, Tue–Sat 6.30–9.30pm; $$$-$$$$

The menu reflects an Italian-Asian marriage – Venice-born Oscar Pasinato cooks while his Singaporean wife Tracy serves – with signatures such as tofu and vegetable tower, spaghetti with spicy crabmeat and prawns, and Horlicks ice cream. The tiny no-frills seven-table restaurant is always full. Call at least two weeks ahead for dinner reservations.

Pasta Brava

11 Craig Rd; tel: 6227 7550; www.pastabrava.com.sg; Mon–Sat noon–2.30pm and 6.30–10.30pm; $$$-$$$$

Located in an old shophouse, the restaurant's setting is rustic, cosy and reminiscent of a traditional Italian home. Affable chef-owner Rolando Luceri ensures that guests feel right at home. Dig into grilled vegetable-based antipasti before enjoying delicious home-made pastas like ravioli stuffed with pumpkin and draped in red pepper and cream sauce.

Thai

Thanying

2/F, Amara Hotel, 165 Tanjong Pagar Road; tel: 6222 4688; daily 11.30am–3pm and 6.30–10pm; $$$

This established restaurant serves authentic royal Thai cuisine. The green curry is excellent, as are the stuffed chicken wings and minced shrimp grilled on a stick of sugar cane and the fragrant olive rice. Be sure to leave room for the delicious dessert buffet.

Orchard Road

Chinese

Din Tai Fung

290 Orchard Rd., B1-03/06 Paragon; tel: 6836-8336; daily 10am–11pm; $$-$$$

This popular restaurant is always crowded during meal times so queuing may be necessary. Feast on the famous *xiao long bao*, or steamed pork dumplings, and other delicious dishes such as the prawn wonton with chilli oil and wholesome chicken soup.

French

Les Amis

02-16 Shaw Centre, 1 Scotts Road; tel: 6733 2225; www.lesamis. com.sg; Mon–Sat noon–2pm and 7–9.30pm; $$$$

This sophisticated restaurant draws well-heeled diners with its exquisite French cuisine, which is light and contemporary with a focus on natural flavours. The award-winning wine list of some 2,000 labels is outstanding. The chic main dining room is illuminated by three antique Parisian chandeliers.

Indonesian

The Rice Table

02-09 International Building, 360 Orchard Road; tel: 6835 3783; www.ricetable.com.sg; daily noon–3.00pm and 6–9.15 pm; $

Diners love this place for its reasonably priced and substantial *rijstaffel* buffet

Above from far left: Coriander Leaf; Da Paolo.

Buffets
It's common to see Singaporeans making a beeline for buffets. Some of the best ones are located in upscale hotels, such as The Line (tel: 6213 4275) at Shangri-La hotel and Melt (tel: 6885 3082) at Mandarin Oriental. Both restaurants serve a superb smorgasbord of Asian and International favourites plus decadent dessert spreads. Also worth considering is mezza9 (tel: 6732 1234) at the Grand Hyatt. Choose from nine different food and beverage concepts, including a Western grill and rotisserie, sushi and sashimi bar, crustacean bar and European deli. The Sunday brunch with free-flow champagne is especially popular among expats.

Dining Hotspots

Discover some of Singapore's off-the-beaten-track dining enclaves such as Rochester Park, once the home of British officers. Located in western Singapore, the area's black-and-white colonial-era bungalows have been taken over by hip F&B outlets surrounded by lush greenery. Another popular area is Tanglin Village. Here, British army barracks have been transformed into a slew of trendy restaurants, wine bars and gourmet food shops.

brought straight to the table. Indonesian dishes such as *tahu telor* (tofu omelette), beef *rendang* (spicy beef stew), grilled chicken and satay are firm favourites.

Singaporean
Chatterbox

Meritus Mandarin, 333 Orchard Road; tel: 6831 6288; www.mandarin-singapore.com; Sun–Thurs 10am–1am, Fri-Sat 10am–2am; $$$

The iconic coffee house is most famous for its succulent chicken rice – albeit expensive, it is worth a try. The other local specialties such as *nasi lemak* (coconut rice with sambal and other condiments) and lobster *laksa* are great for those who like spicy dishes.

Straits Kitchen

Grand Hyatt Singapore, 10 Scotts Road; tel: 6732 1234; daily 6.30pm–midnight; $$$$

Local favourites are served buffet-style at this upscale restaurant. Take your pick from the Indian, Chinese and Malay theatre-kitchens where you can watch chefs whip up your dishes. Highly recommended are the grilled char *kway teow* (fried rice noodles), *laksa* and satay.

Price guide for a meal for one (excluding drinks and taxes):

$$$$	over S$50
$$$	S$30–50
$$	S$10–30
$	below S$10

Botanic Gardens and Tanglin Village

European
PS Café

28B Harding Road; tel: 9070 8782; www.pscafe.sg; Mon–Fri 11.30am–5pm, Sat–Sun 9.30am–5pm, Sun–Thurs 6.30pm–midnight, Fri–Sat 6.30pm–2am; $$$

PS Café is a popular meeting place for the trendy crowd. Lighter fare like salads and fish & chips are served during lunch, and more hearty offerings such as beef, mushroom and bacon ragout, and rosemary kofta curry are dished up for dinner. The cakes are scrumptious and the banana mango crumble is divine.

The White Rabbit

39C Harding Road; tel: 6473 9965; Tue–Fri noon–2.30pm, Sat–Sun 10.30am–2.30pm, Tue–Sun 6.30–10.30pm; $$$$

This charming restaurant-bar is housed in a beautifully restored chapel. Tuck into classic European comfort food such as wild mushroom risotto, macaroni and cheese with truffle sauce and black truffle shavings, as well as black forest cake with a twist.

French
Au Jardin

EJH Corner House, Botanic Gardens Visitor Centre, 1 Cluny Road; tel: 6466 8812; www.lesamis.com.sg; Fri 11.30am–3pm, Mon–Sun 7pm– midnight, Sunday brunch 11.30am–3pm; $$$$

Award-winning contemporary French haute cuisine is served in a wonderfully elegant 1920s colonial house overlooking the lush Botanic Gardens. Prior booking for the fixed-priced menu degustation is de rigueur. Its Sunday brunch is also wildly popular. The sommelier will recommend a fine wine to compliment your meal.

Kampong Glam

Malay
Tepak Sireh Restoran

73 Sultan Gate; tel: 6396 4373; www.tepaksireh.com.sg; Mon–Sun 11.30am–2.30pm and 6.30–10pm; $$

This resplendent mustard-coloured building was built more than 150 years ago and was home to Malay royalty. The restaurant's recipes, reportedly handed down from generations, live up to expectations. It serves only buffet-style meals; recommended are its spicy and tender beef *rendang* and *gulai sotong* (squid curry).

Little India

Indian
Muthu's Curry

138 Race Course Road; tel: 6392 1722; www.muthuscurry.com; daily 10am–10pm; $$

This restaurant serves a potent fish-head curry – its award-winning speciality – as well as South Indian dishes such as masala chicken and mutton chops cooked in tomato puree and spices – all served on banana leaves. Forget the cutlery and eat with your fingers.

The East Coast

Seafood
Jumbo Seafood

01-07/08, 1206 East Coast Parkway; tel: 6442 3435; www.jumboseafood.com.sg; daily 5pm–midnight; $$$

Book in advance if you want to get a table. Outstanding dishes are the chilli crabs, pepper crabs and prawns sautéed with oat cereal, curry leaves and chilli. Ask for an alfresco table facing the sea.

Red House Seafood

Block 1204 East Coast Parkway, 01-05; tel: 6442 3112; www.redhouseseafood.com; Mon–Fri 4pm–11.30pm, Sat-Sun 11.30am–11.30pm; $$$

There are several highly popular seafood restaurants at the East Coast Seafood Centre along the East Coast Parkway. Red House is one of them, offering informal outdoor seafood dining. Dishes like chilli crab and drunken prawns are always fresh and lip-smacking.

Sentosa

Osia

Resorts World Sentosa, Crockfords Tower, Level 2, tel: 6577 6560; www.rwsentosa.com; daily noon–3pm, Sun–Wed 6–10pm, Thur–Sat 10.30pm; $$$$

Australian celebrity chef Scott Webster creates a menu inspired by fresh Aussie produce and Asian influences. Osia's signature dishes include the refreshing 'Seafood Ice Experience', Mulwarra lamb rack and shank, and Valrhona hot chocolate soup.

Above from far left: the White Rabbit's classy setup in a former chapel; beautifully presented French modern fare at Au Jardin.

Crab Culture
Chilli crab is considered Singapore's unofficial national dish. Giant, succulent Sri Lankan crabs are smothered in a thick, tangy gravy spiced with galangal, ginger, turmeric and chillies. To give it a good balance, tomatoes are added and finally, beaten egg is swirled into the sauce to thicken it. Most restaurants serve chilli crab with deep-fried *mantou* (Chinese buns) or sliced baguette. Black pepper crabs, tossed in a peppery sauce, are just as popular.

Civic District

Bar Opiume
Asian Civilisations Museum, 1 Empress Place; tel: 6339 2876; www. indochine.com.sg; Mon–Thur 5pm– 2am, Fri–Sat until 3am, Sun until 1am
This bar draws a hip crowd to its jasmine-incensed minimalist interior and huge terrace; ideal for taking in the CBD skyline and river scenes.

New Asia Bar
Level 71, Swissôtel The Stamford, 2 Stamford Road; tel: 6837 3322; www.equinoxcomplex.com; Sun–Tue 3pm–1am, Wed–Thur until 2am, Fri–Sat until 3am
A huge selection of cocktails and wines, and the best uninterrupted views of the city. City Space on the 70th floor is a classy bar with plush sofas and live jazz.

Marina Bay

Ku De Ta
SkyPark at Marina Bay Sands North Tower, 1 Bayfront Avenue; tel: 6688 7688; www.kudeta.com.sg; SkyBar noon till late daily, Club Lounge 6pm until late daily, SkyDeck 10am until late daily, Poolside Terrace 8am until 10pm daily
The stunning rooftop setting with the best views in town is a must-visit, whether you're after dining, drinking or just entertainment.

Post Bar
The Fullerton Hotel, 1 Fullerton Square; tel: 6877 8135; www.fullerton hotel.com; Mon–Fri, noon–midnight, Sat 5pm–2am, Sun 3pm–2am
This trendy bar serves a fine selection of martinis and signature cocktails. The ceiling and pillars of the former General Post Office have been incorporated into a sophisticated and modern interior.

Singapore River

Archipelago Craft Beer Hub
79 Circular Road, Boat Quay; tel: 6327 8408; www.archipelago brewery.com; Mon–Fri 2pm–1am, Sat 3pm–3am, Sun 3pm–1am
Handcrafted wheat beers and ales with Asian flavours (think palm sugar and coconut milk, tamarind and lemon-grass) by its creative and award-winning American brewmaster Fal Allen.

Attica
01-03 Clarke Quay, 3A River Valley Road; tel: 6333 9973; www.attica. com.sg; Sun–Tue 5pm–2am, Thur until 3am, Wed, Fri–Sat until 4am
Attica features a main bar, which is the focal point joining the dance floor to VIP spaces and a courtyard with a lush Balinese garden setting. Latino, jazz and funk is played at this sexy joint. Check out the alfresco bar on the 'lily-pad' seats just by the river's edge.

Highlander Bar
01-11 Clarke Quay, 3B River Valley Road; tel: 6235 9528; www.highland erasia.com; Sun–Thur 5pm–2am, Fri–Sat, public holiday evenings 5pm–3am
This bar recreates the atmosphere of a Scottish castle with wood panelling and barrelheads on a stone wall. A glass display lined with 200 types of whiskies is a sight to behold.

Zouk

17 Jiak Kim Street, tel. 6738 2988; www.zoukclub.com; Zouk open Wed, Fri–Sat 10pm–late, Phuture open Wed, Fri–Sat 9pm–late Velvet Underground open Wed–Sat 9pm–late, Wine Bar open Tues 6pm–2am, Wed–Thur 6pm–3am, Fri–Sat 6pm–4am

One of Singapore's iconic clubs has regular appearances by celebrity DJs. Also houses the chill-out Wine Bar and the more intimate Velvet Underground.

Orchard Road

Alley Bar

Peranakan Place, 180 Orchard Road; tel: 6738 8818; www.peranakan place.com; Sun–Thur 5pm–2am, Fri–Sat, public holiday evenings until 3am

A back alley was transformed into this hip hangout, which draws yuppies to its black terrazzo bar for cocktails such as mojitos and margaritas.

Balaclava

2 Orchard Turn, ION Orchard; #05-02; tel: 6634 8377; www.imaginings.com.sg; Mon–Thur 3pm–1am, Fri, Sat, public holiday evenings, until 2am, Sun, until 11pm

This bar has great live music, a stylish crowd and an ultra-chic decor to match.

Ice Cold Beer

9 Emerald Hill; tel: 6735 9929; www.emeraldhillgroup.com; Sun–Thur 5pm–2am, Fri–Sat until 3am

Occupying a shophouse built in 1910, this bar has ice tanks to ensure that its 50 types of beers are chilled to the right temperature in under 10 minutes. Its 9-inch hotdogs are incredibly good.

Tanglin Village

Hacienda

13A Dempsey Road; tel: 6476 2922; www.hacienda.com.sg; Sun–Thur 5pm–1am, Fri–Sat, public holiday evenings until 2am

Chill out on the open-air deck or in a leafy courtyard of this restored villa while you sip a watermelon martini.

The Wine Company

14D Dempsey Road; tel: 6479 9341; www.thewinecompany.com.sg; Mon–Thur 3pm–midnight, Fri until 1am, Sat noon–1am, Sun noon–11pm

Deep in the heart of Tanglin Village, this gem of a place stocks a fine selection of South African wines paired with complementary snacks.

Southern Singapore

St James Power Station

3 Sentosa Gateway; tel: 6270 7676; www.stjamespowerstation.com; opening hours vary at each venue

There are nine outlets here – Powerhouse dance club; Movida, which plays Afro-Cuban and world music; and Bellini Room for live swing and jazz.

Tanjong Beach Club

120 Tanjong Beach Walk; tel: 6270 1355; www.tanjongbeachclub.com; Tue–Thur 11am–11pm, Fri 11am–1am, Sat 10am–1am, Sun 10am–midnight

Escape from the hustle and bustle of the city at this all-day beach hideout.

CREDITS

Insight Step by Step Singapore
Written and updated by: Amy Van
Layout by: Derrick Lim
Series Editor: Carine Tracanelli
Cartography Editors: James Macdonald, Zoë Goodwin
Picture Manager: Steven Lawrence
Art Editor: Ian Spick
Photography by: Apa: Jeremy Hou, Jonathan Koh, Jack Hollingsworth, Derrick Lim, Tan Kok Yong, Tony Ying, Low Jat Leng, Ingo Jezierski Vincent Ng except: Alain Compost 91TL; Alain Evrard 34B; Apa Archives 2/3, 23, 31TL; The Arts House 29T; Asian Civilisations Museum 10B, 28T; Civil Aviation Authority of Singapore 12TL, 107; Coriander Leaf 120; Eric Damagnez/Singapore GP Pte Ltd 41M; Four Seasons 113R; Front Row 53B; Fullerton Hotel 24CTL, 96CB; Grand Copthorne Waterfront 112L; Inagiku 119L&R; IndoChine Group 20T, 96CBR, 116; Jamie Koh 84T; Javad Namazie/Pluck 67B; Joseph R. Yogerst 79; Jurong BirdPark 2CBL, 4C, 80L&R; Les Amis Group 120-121; Marina Mandarin 96CT, 112; Meritus Mandarin 111; Mint Museum of Toys 31B; National Museum of Singapore 7BR, 24/25, 35, 36(all); National Parks Board 12TR, 24CBL, 62M, 82M, 90B; New Majestic Hotel 112R; Night Safari 7T, 94/95T, 95TR; One-Ninety 122/123; Peranakan Museum 28M, 33T, 34(all); Pingo/The Shop 29M; Private Archives 22T; Raffles Hotel 2CB, 17B, 31M, 96CTR, 96CBL, 110; Rang Mahal 119R; Rasa Sentosa 96CTL; red dot design museum 49TR&M; Risis Pte Ltd 19B; The Scarlet 113L; Sentosa 2CBR, 4CTR, 6CT, 24CT, 72(all),73TL, 75T&MT, 76T&B, 77, 78M, 100; The Sentosa Resort & Spa 75MB, 115; Singapore Art Museum 37(all); Singapore Flyer Pte Ltd 8CTR, 10T ; Singapore Tourism Board 2CTL, 4B, 14(all), 16B; Singapore Zoo 93TL, 94TL&M; Swissôtel The Stamford 2CTR; Timbré 21B; True Blue 118L; Tung Lok Seafood 123R; Underwater World Singapore 76M; Watertours Pte Ltd 78T; The White Rabbit 122L
Front Cover: 4Corners (top); Fotolia (bottom left); iStockphoto (bottom right).
Back Cover: APA/Vincent Ng (left and right)
Printed by: CTPS-China

© 2012 Apa Publications GmbH & Co. Verlag KG (Singapore branch)

CONTACTING THE EDITORS

We would appreciate it if readers would alert us to errors or outdated information by writing to us at insight@apaguide.co.uk or Apa Publications, PO Box 7910, London SE1 1WE, UK.

www.insightguides.com

DISTRIBUTION

Worldwide
APA Publications GmbH & Co. Verlag KG
(Singapore branch)
7030 Ang Mo Kio Ave 5
08-65 Northstar @ AMK, Singapore 569880
Email: apasin@singnet.com.sg

UK and Ireland
Dorling Kindersley Ltd,
(a Penguin Company)
80 Strand, London, WC2R 0RL, UK
Email: sales@uk.dk.com

US
Ingram Publisher Services
One Ingram Blvd, PO Box 3006
La Vergne, TN 37086-1986
Email: customer.service@ingrampublisher
services.com

Australia
Universal Publishers
PO Box 307
St. Leonards NSW 1590
Email: sales@universalpublishers.com.au

INDEX

A

Abdul Gaffoor Mosque **69**
accommodation **110–15**
Al Abrar Mosque **49**
Alkaff Bridge **45**
Anderson Bridge **43**
Angullia Mosque **70**
Animal & Bird Encounters
    (Sentosa) **75**
Ann Siang Hill **53**
Arab Street **18, 65**
Armenian Church of
    St Gregory the
    Illuminator **30**
ARTrium **29**
Art Science Museum **41**
Arts House, The **29**
Asian Civilisations Museum
    28–9, 43
Atrium@Orchard, The **59**

B

Bali Lane **67**
Battle Box, The **32–3**
Boat Quay **12, 20, 21, 43**
Buddha Tooth Relic Temple
    and Museum **52–3**
Buddhist Culture Museum
    (Buddha Tooth Relic
    Temple and Museum) **53**
Bukit Timah Hill **91**
Bukit Timah Nature Reserve
    91–2
business hours **98**
Bussorah Street **65**
Butterfly Park & Insect
    Kingdom (Sentosa) **74**

C

Campbell Lane **68**
Capital Square **48**
Cathedral of the Good
    Shepherd **30**

Cavenagh Bridge **43**
Cenotaph **39**
Central, The **44**
Central Business District **46–9**
Central Fire Station **29–30**
Centrepoint **59**
Changi **88–90**
Changi Beach Park **90**
Changi Chapel and Museum
    88–9
Changi Massacre Site **90**
Changi Point Ferry Terminal
    90
Changi Village **89–90**
Chijmes **30–1**
children **98**
Chinatown **12, 19, 50–53**
Chinatown Complex **51–2**
Chinatown Food Street **52**
Chinatown Heritage Centre **51**
Chinatown Night Market **19,
    51**
Chinese Garden **81**
Chinese Opera Teahouse **52**
Church of the Holy Family
    86
City Hall **27**
CityLink Mall **18, 26**
city overview **10–13**
Civic District **26–31**
Civil Defence Heritage
    Gallery **30**
Clarke Quay **20, 21, 43,
    44–5**
climate **98**
clothing **99**
Coleman Bridge **44**
Collyer Quay **40–1**
Crawford, John **26**
customs **99**
Customs House **41**

D

Dempsey **63**
Dempsey Hill **20**

DFS Galleria **55**
Dhoby Ghaut **59**
disabled travellers **99**
Dolphin Lagoon (Sentosa) **75**
Dunlop Street **69**

E

East Coast Seafood
    Centre **87**
East Coast Park **85–7**
East Coast Road **85**
electricity **100**
Elgin Bridge **44**
embassies **99**
Emerald Hill **20, 58**
emergencies **100**
Esplanade Concert Hall **21**
Esplanade Mall **18, 39–40**
Esplanade Park **39**
Esplanade – Theatres on the
    Bay, The **23, 38–39**
etiquette **100**
Eurasian Heritage Centre **85**
Eu Yan Sang **50**

F

Far East Plaza **18, 56**
Far East Square **48**
festivals **100**
food and drink **14–17**
Formula 1 Singapore
    Grand Prix **23, 41**
Fort Canning Hill **33**
Fort Canning Park **29, 32**
Fort Siloso (Sentosa) **76–7**
Forum The Shopping Mall
    18, 55
Fountain of Wealth **38**
Fullerton Heritage **41**
Fullerton Hotel **21, 40**
Fullerton Waterboat House
    39–40
Funan DigitaLife Mall **18**
Fu Tak Chi Museum **48**

G

gay/lesbian **101**
Gedung Kuning **66**
Goh, Chok Tong **11, 23**
Goodwood Park Hotel **56**
government **101**
Grand Hyatt **56**
Great Singapore Sale **18**

H

Haji Lane **18, 66–7**
Hajjah Fatimah Mosque
 66
hawker centres **17**
Haw Par Villa **83**
health **101**
Heeren Shops, The **18, 57**
Helix Bridge **41**
Hilton Hotel **18, 55**
history **22–3**

I

ifly Singapore **75**
Images of Singapore (Sentosa)
 75
Imbiah Lookout (Sentosa)
 74
internet **102**
ION Orchard **57**
Istana **59**
Istana Kampong Gelam **66**
Istana Park **59**

J

Jacob Ballas Children's Garden
 (Singapore Botanic
 Gardens) **62**
Jamae Mosque **50**
Japanese Garden **81**
Jewel Box, The **82–3**
Joo Chiat **84–5**
Jubilee Hall **31**
Jurong BirdPark **80–81**
Jurong Lake **81**

K

Kampong Glam **12, 18, 64–7**
Kandahar Street **66**
Katong **84–7**
Katong Antique House **87**
Kim Choo Kueh
 Chang **15, 85–6**
Koon Seng Road **85**
Kuan Im Tng Temple **84–5**
Kusu Island **78–9**

L

Lai Chun Yuen **52**
Lee, Hsien Loong **11, 23**
Lee, Kuan Yew **11, 22–3**
Legends Fort Canning Park
 Country Club, The **33**
Leong San See Temple **71**
Liat Towers **55**
Lim Bo Seng Memorial **39**
Little India **12, 18, 68–71**
Little India Arcade **19, 68**
lost property **102**
Lucky Plaza **57**

M

MacDonald House **59**
Makansutra Gluttons Bay **39,
 59**
Malabar Muslim Jama-Ath
 Mosque **66**
Malay Heritage Centre **66**
Mandai **93–5**
Mandai Orchid Garden **95**
Mandarin Gallery **57**
maps **102**
Marina Bay **38–41**
Marina Bay Promenade **39**
Marina Bay Sands **41**
Marina Square **18, 39**
Market of Artists and
 Designers (MAAD) **49**
Marriott Hotel **57**
Maxwell Food Centre **53**
media **102**

Merlion (Sentosa) **74**
Merlion Park **40**
MICA Building **29**
Minden Road **63**
Mint Museum of Toys **31**
money **103**
Mosque Street **51**
Mount Faber **82–3**
museum district **32–7**
Mustafa Centre **18, 70**

N

Nagore Durgha Building **48**
National Art Gallery **27**
National Museum **35–6**
National Orchid Garden **61–2**
Nature Walk (Sentosa) **75**
New Supreme Court **27, 43**
Ngee Ann City **18, 57**
nightlife **20–21, 122–3**
Night Safari **94–5**

O

OCBC Centre **47**
Old Supreme Court **27**
One Fullerton **40**
Orchard Central **59**
Orchard Road **18, 20, 54–9**

P

Padang **26–7**
Pagoda Street **51**
Palais Renaissance **18, 55**
Palawan Beach (Sentosa) **75**
Paragon, The **18, 57**
Parliament House **29**
Peranakan Museum **28, 33–4**
Peranakan Place **58**
Peranakans **15–16, 34**
photography **103**
Plaza Singapura **59**
postal services **104**
public holidays **104**
Pulau Hantu **79**
Pulau Ubin **90**

R

Race Course Road **71**
Raffles, Thomas Stamford **10, 22, 26, 28, 33, 50, 60, 64, 68**
Raffles Hotel **21, 31**
Raffles Hotel Shopping Arcade **18, 31**
Raffles City **18, 26**
Raffles' Landing Site **28–9, 43**
Raffles Place **46**
Read Bridge **44**
red dot design museum **49**
red dot Traffic **49**
religion **104**
Republic Plaza **47**
Resorts World Sentosa **72–3**
restaurants **116–21**
Riverside Point **44**
Robertson Quay **43, 45**
Robinsons **59**
Rumah Bebe **86**

S

Sands Sky Park **41**
Sago Street **52**
St Andrew's Cathedral **26**
St Hilda's Anglican Church **85**
St James Power Station **20, 83**
St John's Island **79**
Sakya Muni Buddha Gaya Temple **71**
Science Centre **81**
Seletar Reservoir **92**
Sentosa **20, 72–7**
Sentosa CineBlast **74**
Sentosa 4D Magix **74**
Serangoon Road **18, 68**
Shaw Centre **55**
Shaw Foundation Symphony Stage **61**
shopping **18–19**
Siloso Beach (Sentosa) **75**
Singapore Art Museum **37**
Singapore Botanic Gardens **60–62**

Singapore City Gallery **53**
Singapore Cricket Club **27**
Singapore Flyer **23, 40**
Singapore Island Cruises **78**
Singapore Philatelic Museum **33**
Singapore Recreation Club **27**
Singapore River **42–5**
Singapore Sling **21, 31**
Singapore Symphony Orchestra **21, 38**
Singapore Tyler Print Institute **45**
Singapore Visitors Centre **58, 105**
Singapore Zoo **93–4**
Sisters' Island **79**
Skyline Luge Sentosa **74**
Smith Street **52**
smoking **105**
Songs of the Sea (Sentosa) **77**
Southern Islands **78–9**
Southern Ridges **82**
sports **87, 104**
Sri Mariamman Temple **50–51**
Sri Senpaga Vinayagar Temple **85**
Sri Srinivasa Perumal Temple **70**
Sri Veeramakaliamman Temple **69**
Stamford House **32**
Substation, The **34**
Sultan Mosque **65–6**
Suntec City **38**
Suntec City Mall **18, 38**
Syed Alwi Road **70**

T

TANGS department store **57**
Tanglin Mall **54**
Tanglin Road **54–5**
Tanglin Shopping Centre **18, 55**
Tanglin Village **62–3**

Tanjong Beach (Sentosa) **75**
Tanjong Pagar **12**
Tan Kim Seng Fountain **39**
telephones **105**
Telok Ayer Chinese Methodist Church **49**
Telok Ayer Street **48–9**
Thaipusam **70–71, 100**
Thian Hock Kian Temple **49**
Tiger Sky Tower (Sentosa) **74**
toilets **106**
tourist information **105**
tours **105**
transport **106–8**
Trengganu Street **51**
Tua Pek Kong Temple (Kusu Island) **79**
Tudor Court **55**

U

UOB Plaza **47**
Underwater World (Sentosa) **76**
Universal Studios Singapore **73**

V

Vanda Miss Joaquim **30, 62**
Victoria Concert Hall **27–8**
Victoria Theatre **27–8**
visas and passports **109**
VivoCity **83**

W

Wak Hai Cheng Temple **47–8**
Warehouse Sentosa **75**
Waterboat House **39**
websites **109**
Wheelock Place **55**
Wisma Atria **57**

X/Y/Z

Youth Olympic Park **41**
Yue Hwa Emporium **19, 51**
Zouk **21**

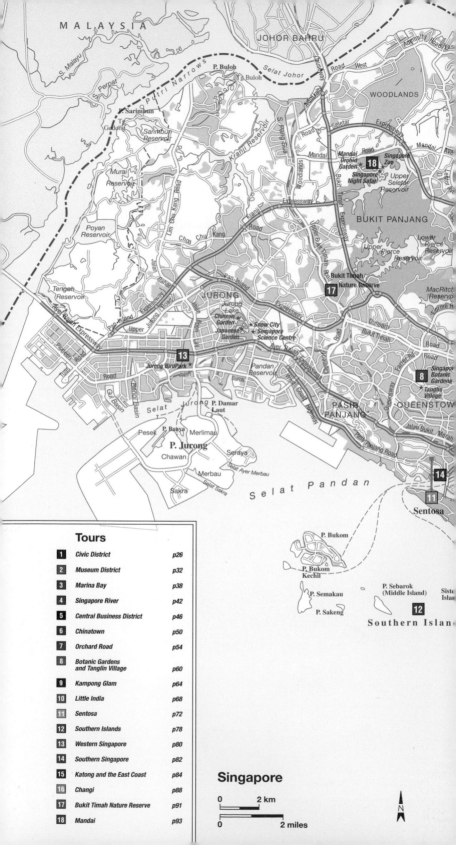

MALAYSIA
JOHOR BAHRU

WOODLANDS

P. Buloh
Selat Johor
P. Buloh

P. Sarimbun
Sarimbun
Reservoir

Murai
Reservoir

Poyan
Reservoir

Tengah
Reservoir

Mandai
Orchid
Garden
Singapore
Night Safari
18
Singapore
Zoo

Upper
Seletar
Reservoir

BUKIT PANJANG

Upper
Pierce
Reservoir

Lower
Pierce
Reservoir

MacRitchie
Reservoir

JURONG
Jurong
Lake
Chinese
Garden
Japanese
Garden

Snow City
Singapore
Science Centre

Bukit Timah
Nature Reserve
17

Bukit Timah

Singapore
Botanic
Gardens
8
Tanglin
Village

QUEENSTOWN

Jurong BirdPark
13

Pandan
Reservoir

PASIR
PANJANG

P. Damar
Laut

Selat Jurong

Pesek P. Buaya Merlimau

Chawan

Seraya

Merbau

Sakra

P. Jurong

Selat Ayer Merbau

14
11
Sentosa

Selat Pandan

P. Bukom

P. Bukom
Kechil

P. Semakau

P. Sakeng

P. Sebarok
(Middle Island)

12

Sister
Island

Southern Islands

Tours

1	Civic District	p26
2	Museum District	p32
3	Marina Bay	p38
4	Singapore River	p42
5	Central Business District	p46
6	Chinatown	p50
7	Orchard Road	p54
8	Botanic Gardens and Tanglin Village	p60
9	Kampong Glam	p64
10	Little India	p68
11	Sentosa	p72
12	Southern Islands	p78
13	Western Singapore	p80
14	Southern Singapore	p82
15	Katong and the East Coast	p84
16	Changi	p88
17	Bukit Timah Nature Reserve	p91
18	Mandai	p93

Singapore

0   2 km

0   2 miles

N